From Karnack to Compton:

One Man's Journey and

Presence

Ronald McCowan

To Karen,
We miss seeing you
at memorial. May
God continue to bless
you and your family.
Sincerely,
Ron McCowan
12/19/12

RONALD MCCOWAN

From Karnack to Compton: One Man's Journey and Presence.

For more information, address:
Enaz Publications
P.O. Box 030064
Elmont N.Y. 11003

www.blackbookplus.com

ISBN 1-59232-379-0

Printed in the United States of America

Introduction

A king, realizing his incompetence, can either delegate or abdicate his duties. A father can do neither. If only sons could see the paradox, they would understand the dilemma. —Marlene Dietrich

The writing of this brief biography has been a joyful, but long, road fueled by a nagging need to see it completed and to experience some degree of closure, although, I realize there can be no complete closure with a deceased loved one. The memories of a deceased family member never die, and they sometimes rush forth with such clarity and captivation that we mourn anew. The closure here deals with seeking the opportunity to speak one more time, to ask the questions never asked, and to explain what was never explained.

All is not morose, however, as this literary journey has given me reason for celebration. I have learned a great deal. First, ancestors must be encouraged to tell their story, not only from an historic perspective but from their pathos and ethos.

Second, we listeners must permanently record what's told for the mind is privy to forgetfulness and hyperbole to the point of making historical events fictional. It's

3

fascinating to see the front of someone's Bible filled with names, birth and death dates, and a few descriptive words about cherished individuals.

One of the most difficult challenges in life is to take a panoramic view of the people we love and our relationships with them without any direct input from them. A cast of witnesses is needed. Still, there is a great risk of getting it all wrong. The mere attempt to write the biography, objectively and subjectively, allows one to grow in many ways.

One purpose of this book is to provide background to understanding the origin and inspiration of the Jack Jeffrey McCowan Memorial Scholarship. The scholarship program was started in honor of my father, who was a staunch proponent of education and overcame great odds to get his own education. He understood the power of knowledge and the need for its liberating force in the black community, a subject never far from his lips. The scholarship has been awarded yearly to needy, but academically attentive, students at this school. This scholarship was first awarded in 2003 to two students at the Los Angeles Adventist Academy.

Additionally, I spent my first eight years of elementary and junior high school education at this

4

institution in the 1960s when it was called Los Angeles Union Seventh-Day Adventist school. I recall this institution in South Central Los Angeles being comprised of teachers who were concerned about students having a well-rounded education and took time to teach them about life, as well as the required academic subjects; moreover, the emphasis on a Christ-centered life was paramount.

Over the years, the uniqueness of the institution and its extended family has provided examples of effective socialization with great warmth and depth. This extended family is comprised of the many teachers, administrators, parents, friends, and former students. This gift of socialization is shared yearly through a weekend reunion at the school, during which old friendships are rekindled and new ones forged.

Like most schools, one challenge has been tapping into the resources of the extended family. The vision, mission, and efforts exist, and through fully committed, strong, and charismatic leadership, sizeable returns are likely to be seen. The Los Angeles Adventist Academy (LAAA) Alumni Association, established in 2009, has made great strides to reach these goals through membership dues and fund-raising events, but more individual contributions are needed. For a former student, this would be a wonderful way to say *thank you* for a profound experience and education. Personally, I am truly grateful for the contribution this school made, not only to my education and life, but to the many other students who passed through the "halls of Union."

An additional reason for writing this book is to preserve some family history. The oral tradition, the job of the old West African storytellers, known as griots, is alive and well in many African communities. These historians tell their stories often through poetry and singing with the aid of musical instruments. They are required to master seven generations of a tribe's or family's history. A daunting task. Not having the mind or training of a griot, I have written what I've learned as quickly as I learned it. A wise, old man told me, "The mind is like a sieve with more things passing through it than are retained."

In May of 2008, Joshua Alston wrote an article entitled, "O Father, Where Art Thou?" in which he said, "The engaged black father is an elusive character in popular culture. The percentage of black children living in fatherless homes–roughly 50 %–has perpetuated the orthodoxy that black men are irresponsible and indifferent to fatherhood."

The popular "Maury Show" promotes this image with its parade of black men, crowned as deadbeat dads, awaiting paternity tests.

Alston added, "A 2007 study noted a black father's ability to financially contribute is one of the biggest determinants of whether he stays in the home," but on the other hand "Black fathers who don't reside in the home are more likely to sustain regular contact with their children than fathers of any other racial group." [1] This latter statement speaks of a positive presence, a challenge to create if a divorce or another breach in the family has occurred.

I was blessed to have a father who not only lived with us, but was involved with us. For me, he had a presence that extended well beyond his personal space, our home, and his sixty-three years. That which we do and say as a parent, for good or bad, verbally and otherwise, creates an incredibly powerful influence on the child. This influence can travel amazingly far in distance and time.

Finally, I'm grateful for my father's siblings, Aunt Ruby (RIP) and Uncle Mack, and their help in filling in information gaps about my father's childhood and the environment in which they were raised.

I would, also, like to thank my mother, Barbara McCowan-Williams for her information concerning my father's and her life. My father would not have been successful and an overcomer without her personal sacrifices, wisdom, and care. And for her help, thank you to my sister, Angela Van Buren, who enjoyed a close relationship with our father.

I have been blessed with a beautiful, loving, and supportive wife, Karlene, who encouraged me to finish this work. I am appreciative of her. And to our children Brittany, Brandon, and Ryan, what a blessing and source of growth they have been.

I am also grateful for you, the reader, for reading this book. Hopefully the content will interest and inspire you.

To our Heavenly Father, I give praise and honor for His grace and sustaining power, without which I would not have completed this task. Without Him there is no life, success, prosperity, or health, for it is written that *every good gift and every perfect gift is from above, and cometh down from the Father of lights.* (James 1:17)

Chapter 1 – The Times

Stand ye in the ways, and see, and ask for the old paths, where is the good way, and walk therein, and ye shall find rest for your souls. —Jeremiah 6:16.

While this verse specifically addresses the need for Judah and mankind to return to God's established ways, it also emphasizes in a general sense the importance of learning and making life applications from history so one's life might be less cumbersome because of learning an established and proven way of living. So we stand in the ways, and see, and ask for the old paths.

I have wondered what life was like in the U.S. South during the 1930s. What was life like for a colored, Negro, black, or African American person? One can choose whichever moniker, but in this decision moving to the right, away from colored, and toward black is progressive, in my opinion.

A brief historical journey will help us get a sense of life in those times and may help us appreciate the mindset, struggles, and motivations experienced by its people.

My father was born in Marshall, Texas, on November 9, 1931, the last of six children of Bertha and Albert McCowan. As expected, there was no rushing to a local hospital for labor and delivery care. The community midwife was the only option and a satisfactory one.

According to the online Handbook of Texas, a State Bureau of Child Hygiene survey estimated at least 4,000 midwives were practicing in Texas in 1924. The midwives were usually older women who learned their vocation through apprenticeships with other midwives and primarily served rural populations, especially in the eastern and southern part of the state. (1) By the late 1930s, only half of U.S. births occurred in a hospital with the rest attended by midwives in a home setting.

The midwife delivering my father would have been black. I found no stories of an umbilical cord wrapped
10

around the neck, or breech birth, or a blue baby, just a normal, healthy baby boy, screaming at the top of his lungs, soon wrapped in a warm blanket and cuddled.

The majority of U.S. hospitals did not admit blacks for care during the 1930s and didn't do so until after 1965. Title VI of the Civil Rights Act of 1964 and Title XVIII of the Social Security Amendments of 1965 (Medicare) greatly influenced hospitals to integrate, due to the legal and economic implications. The transition from segregated to nonsegregated hospitals was not a smooth, friendly, overnight operation.

During the 1930s in the U.S., notable and colorful characters made their presences known, and a few current consumer products had their beginnings. Al Capone, "Scarface," the one who said, "I own Chicago," and the most famous mobster of that era, was sentenced in 1932 to eleven years in prison for tax evasion and was paroled in 1939. His notoriety still looms large today, for his gun, a colt 0.38 manufactured in 1929, recently was sold in London for $108,447.

James Earl Jones, the actor and voice of Darth Vader from the "Star Wars" movies and Mustafa of "The Lion King," was born in January 1931. He also overcame a major stuttering problem.

Barbara Walters, the first anchorperson to earn a yearly million dollars and co-host of the popular morning show "The View," was born September 1931 in Boston, Massachusetts.

Alka Seltzer, the pain reliever and antacid, with its notable marketing slogan "Plop, plop, fizz, fizz; oh, what a relief it is," was first available in 1931. (2)

As a relief to those plagued with graying tops, Clairol hair color was enthusiastically introduced to the U.S. in 1931 by Lawrence M. Gelb, a chemist from New York.

The Fisher-Price Toy Company was founded in 1930. Herman Fisher, Irving Price, and Helen Schelle formed this company and subsequently presented sixteen wooden toys to the International Toy Fair in New York City. (3)

Thomas Edison, the famous inventor known for originating the phonograph and improving the light bulb, died in 1928 at the age of 80. He had hired a black draftsman by the name of Lewis Latimer to work for him. Latimer had invented and patented a "pivot bottom" for water closets on trains in 1874 and published a book entitled *Incandescent Electric Lighting* in 1896.(4)

Black politicians were sparse during this time period. In 1929 Oscar DePriest, a black republican from Chicago, became the first U.S. congressman since 1900 when

George Henry White served as a republican from North Carolina. He was successful in getting bills passed that sent congressional funds to Howard University and appointments of blacks to the U.S. Military Academy at West Point. However, he was known for not supporting aid to the poor or taxation of the rich. (4) He would fit in nicely with his modern day conservative counterparts.

William Dawson, who unseated DePriest in 1934, was the first black democrat elected to the U.S. congress.

First Lady Eleanor Roosevelt recruited educator and women's rights activist, Mary McLeod Bethune, as a member of the Black Cabinet, first known as the Federal Council of Negro Affairs, in 1936. Bethune was best known for starting a school for black students in Daytona Beach, Florida. She started a school for black girls there and in 1923 merged it with Cookman College of Jacksonville to become the Bethune-Cookman School and later Bethune-Cookman University. It was considered a quality university with high education standards. Bethune was president of the college until 1942.

When considering blacks and sports in the 1930s, one must think of Andrew "Rube" Foster, who formed the Negro National League, comprised of eight baseball teams.

This professional league flourished until the 1950s when players such as Jackie Robinson, the first black to go to Major League Baseball, Larry Doby, Hank Aaron, Ernie Banks, Willie Mays, and many others were able to transition to Major League Baseball.

The Negro League ended in 1962. Of interest, some have advocated the need to resurrect the Negro League in response to the current declining number of black players in Major League Baseball. (5)

Blacks in the 1930s listened to music that included the blues of Bessie Smith, the jazz of Charlie Parker, Louis Armstrong, Ella Fitzgerald, Duke Ellington, Count Basie, Jellie Roll Morton, and others, and the gospel music of Thomas Dorsey, Sallie Martin, and Willie Mae Ford Smith.

The music of that era lives on and serves as standards and lesson books for the novice and professional. The Charlie Parker Omnibook, a compilation of sixty of Parker's songs transcribed by Jamey Aebersold and Ken Slone, has served as a bible of bebop improvisation to many budding jazz artists since its publication in 1978.

Life expectancy in the U.S. during the 1930s was 59.7 years, compared to the 77.6 years, based on 2005 estimates. (6) This improvement in longevity has been

14

attributed to advancements in disease treatment, the emphasis on prevention, and consumers taking an active role in their own health maintenance. Some have projected even greater magnitudes of increased longevity over time. Currently, the longest living persons in the U.S. reside in Loma Linda, CA.

These added years are thought due to a lifestyle of abstinence from smoking and drinking, regular exercise, a diet of little or no meat products, plenty of nuts, having a normal-body index, and a spiritual emphasis, which includes a weekly rest day, the biblical seventh day Sabbath. (7)

According to Dan Buettner, there are other areas in the world with similar longevity including Okinawa, Japan, Sardinia, Italy, Nicoya, Costa Rica, and Ikaria, Greece. Regular church attendance has, also, been shown to be associated with increased longevity. (8)

In 1931, the most common cause of death was heart disease with 252,000 deaths occurring. Heart disease remains the number one cause of death in the U.S. In 2003, 685,000 deaths were related to this cause. In the 1930s a heart attack was managed with oxygen, narcotics, and a six-week period of bed rest at home. Current management is directed toward opening the affected

15

coronary artery and restoring blood flow as quickly as possible to prevent or minimize loss of heart muscle. To this end, balloon angioplasty, coronary stenting, bypass surgery, thrombolytic (clot busting) drugs, etc. have been developed.

The major heart attack risk factors, such as hypertension, diabetes mellitus, hyperlipidemia, age, male sex, and smoking, were not part of the medical society's prevention agenda in the 1930s. However, the benefits of diminished stress, exercise, and smoking cessation were appreciated by studious health zealots and a few in the health care ranks.

Much has been learned for practical applications. For instance, the Adventist Health Study (9), which in one phase has enrolled more than 30,000 patients, has shown that by not smoking, consuming a plant-based diet, exercising regularly, eating nuts several times per week (10), and maintaining normal body weight, one can increase one's life span up to ten years. Through such measures, one can expect an average reduction of coronary artery disease by 30-50%. This lifestyle lowered death rates from lung cancer by 21%, colorectal cancer by 62%, and breast cancer by 85%. (11) These numbers should interest us since cancer is the number two cause of U.S. deaths.

However, the challenges of a lifestyle change must be recognized. In her article entitled, "The High Price for Healthy Food," [12] Tara Parker-Pope said, "Energy-dense munchies cost on average $1.76 per 1,000 calories, compared with $18.16 per 1,000 calories for low-energy, nutritious foods." Furthermore, "low-calorie foods were more likely to increase in price, surging 19.5%" while "high-calorie foods remained a relative bargain, dropping in price by 1.8%." Junk food prices are not affected by inflation to the degree that fruits and vegetables are.

In a University of Washington study, Dr. Adam Drewnowski noted that a 2,000-calorie, junk-food diet would cost about $3.52 a day while a healthy diet of 2,000 calories would be $36.32 a day.

On the other hand, Andrew McDermott [13], in using a single-parent, low income with no-government-assistance model, showed that a healthy diet could cost half as much as an unhealthy diet annually if people would dine out less.

Bottom line, we can all eat more healthy without a major increase in cost if we fix our food at home. More can be said on this issue, but let's move on.

In 1931, unemployment had reached 8 million, the average annual income was $1,858, and a new car cost an average of $640; however, one could spend $15,000 on a new, top-of-the-line, Cadillac, V-16, Town Brougham. Being more economical one could spend $395 for a Model A Ford with a top speed of 65 mph and gas mileage of 20–30 miles per gallon. Gasoline would cost a mere 10¢ per gallon, which seems an impossibility compared to current gas prices.

The McCowan family did not own a car. My father's oldest brother, Addis, known as Spend, bought a car when he was seventeen. This functioned as the family car for two years. When Uncle Spend married, his car moved with him. Issues dealing with no transportation arose. Without the option of borrowing a car, paying someone for transport, a horse and buggy, a bicycle, skate board or otherwise, access to necessities is challenged. Transitioning to a horse and buggy was the painful McCowan option.

The price of the postage stamp in the 1930s was 2¢ (14). While stamps may have been a mundane topic to some the post office murals were engaging. During these times, U.S. post offices and other public buildings painted their walls with murals depicting historical aspects of American life.

To this end, the federal government sought to remedy the ill effects of the Depression era on American morale by creating agencies to support the arts and provide jobs for artists. Over 5,000 jobs were created for artists with over 225,000 works of art produced for Americans. (15) Sometimes the commissioned art work aroused the ire of postal patrons with the excessive display of breasts and buttocks or a scene of "savages" scalping two women. (16) Artists had to make subsequent "adjustments" to their work.

Many murals from that period have survived and been renovated. They offer unique insight into the resolve of Americans not to let the economic burden of that time destroy their dreams and aspirations. Black artists such as Aaron Douglas, referred to as the "Father of African American arts," and the best known artist of the Harlem Renaissance, painted a now well-known mural in 1934 entitled *Aspects of Negro Life,* which can be seen at the Countee Cullen Branch of the New York Public Library. (4) Other famous black muralists during that time included Hale Woodruff, Charles White, and Charles Alston.

The 1929 stock market crash ushered in the Great Depression, which lasted until the 1940s. Someone has to be blamed for the economic disaster of the 1930s.

In 1929, Herbert Hoover, who graduated from Stanford University with a mine engineering degree and served as Secretary of Commerce under Presidents Harding and Coolidge, became the thirty-first President of the United States. In 1931, he declared the Star Spangled Banner our national anthem, but, unfortunately, he became the scapegoat for the Depression era and was defeated in his 1932 re-election effort.[17] His legacy, according to some, is having the reputation of the most unpopular President in the history of the U.S.

Hoover became unpopular with blacks during his tenure as Secretary of Commerce because of his less-than-honorable response to the Mississippi flood of 1927, in which local officials brutalized blacks, prevented them from leaving relief camps, and forced some into labor at gun point. [18]

Chris Edwards, director of tax policy at Cato Institute, said, "Misguided federal policies caused the downturn that began in 1929, and they prevented the economy from fully recovering for a decade." By today's living standard, these times were marked by deprivation for most Americans.

By 1932, it was believed that 75% of the population lived in poverty. More than 15 million Americans were unemployed. In many U.S. places, the unemployment rates for black Americans were four times greater than those of white Americans. A disparity still remains as the unemployment rate for white Americans at this time is 8.1% while the factor is 16.2% for blacks, 11.9% for Hispanics, and 7% for Asians, according to the May 2011 Bureau of Labor Statistics report. [19]

The socio-economic situation for most black Americans left much to be desired. Those fortunate to have a job held mostly blue collar jobs in environments that had not accepted blacks as equals. The need for jobs and an escape from southern oppression led to the mass movement of an estimated 6 million blacks in the Great Migration (1910–1930) to cities of the North, Midwest, and West of the U.S. These were times when public signs "White only" and "Colored only" successfully divided the races and bolstered many myths, distrust, and continued forms of inequality that remain prevalent today. Ignoring the signs brought a boisterous, embarrassing verbal reprimand at the least, and one might have found himself running from a beating or worse.

I recall seeing "White only" signs on restroom doors of businesses as our family drove through towns in Texas and Arkansas in the 1960s. My realization then was that colored referred to me, and anyone looking like me.

Prior to this time, I don't recall the "colored" issue being brought to my attention. Thank goodness, the designation "colored" on U.S. soil is infrequently heard. I would like it to find its place alongside the dodo bird, dinosaurs, and mammoths, but then we would have to get serious about renaming the National Association for the Advancement of Colored People (NAACP). This unflattering epithet thrusts one back to a time of more overt and astounding racial separation and inequality.

To see the signs of "White only" or "Colored only" made me feel powerless as a youngster and created a new sense of being vigilant about not crossing the line. As I stared at one sign, I recall feeling small, unimportant, and unwanted by the majority.

Recently I found a couple of these signs available on EBay. One sign read "Rest Rooms: white only" and cost $4.99. The other was a railroad sign that read "White only" and cost $9.99; three were available. These could certainly serve as conversation pieces and items of historical interest, but I wouldn't want one. The meager prices of these signs do not testify of the robust power they yielded. The signs' power can be traced back to the Plessy v. Ferguson ruling of the U.S. Supreme Court in May of 1896 in which all but one Supreme Court justice ruled that segregation in America was constitutional.

According to the U.S. Equal Opportunity Commission in 2005, Tyson Foods, the mega food corporation, was sued for having a "White only" sign on one of its bathrooms in its Ashland, Alabama, facility. Keys were distributed to white employees only. [20] Some diehards embrace and refuse to relinquish exclusionary views of superiority, classism, and monoculturalism.

Going to see a movie in the 1930s provided some inconveniences, courtesy of Jim Crow. There was the Buzzard's Roost, which was usually a balcony or gallery assigned to blacks.[21]

My Buzzard's Roost experience came thirty years later when I attended a movie in Texarkana, TX. It was in the 1960s when I and two of my mother's brothers (who were close to my age and who I did not refer to as uncle) entered the back of a theater through an old, white, paint-chipped door. We could have been entering an old

23

warehouse, not a movie theater. We sat on oversized black chairs that were notably dirty. Our area was the balcony and it was difficult to see the screen.

Bored with the movie, I roamed the building and went to the downstairs main lobby, where everything was bright and clean. People milled about. Candy and other delicious edibles were on display. The smell of popcorn caught my senses. It would have been nice to buy some, but I had no money. I had found the lobby a much nicer place than upstairs and didn't notice I was the only black person in the area.

Before I got too far, a tall, white gentleman, dressed in a theatre uniform, yelled at me to get out and that I should know I was not allowed to be there.

I wasn't aware of that. It wasn't clear to me that I wasn't supposed to be there because I was "colored." I retreated, unenthusiastically, but pensively, to the unkempt, dark, seclusion of the Buzzard's Roost or "n_ heaven" as some called it. No one cleaned that place, and if one wanted to have a snack, he had to bring it himself.

The threat of lynching added to the baseline fear many southern black Americans experienced during that time. Gunnar Myrdal, a social economist, stated that the southern states accounted for nine-tenths of all lynchings.

24

Richard Perloff, professor of communication at Cleveland State University, stated that the number of lynchings between 1882 and 1968 approximated 4,742. Seventy-three percent of those involved blacks.

What type of motivation, stamina, courage, self-control, and fear did a black American need to be "successful" during those times? Success might be interpreted as simply staying alive. Consequently black education included instructions on how to survive in the white world.

Some years later I had a more comprehensive view of the meaning behind what went on during that time period. I feel a great deal of appreciation for the black people who had lived then. I reflected on my childhood and seeing the black neighborhood fathers in Compton, CA, go to work every day and come home to their families and keep their families together. These men had experienced the Jim Crow times and more.

I think of the thin, angry but soft-hearted, poetry-writing man who carried his lunch pail to work at General Motors, the now ninety-plus-year-old barber who maintains a great sense of humor, the light-skinned man from New Orleans who whistled loudly for his sons to come home when it got dark, the man who, along with another neighbor, owned a gas station in the neighborhood, and the old mechanic who carried on full conversations with a cigarette flopping in his mouth. On a rare occasion when I, we, stopped playing to hear them talking, we glimpsed the 1930s and displays of courage and fortitude and wisdom. We didn't know it was important to ask about those times but I'm sure it was too painful for them to say much. They had moved on, and life was better, for some.

Through the home, local church, and community, blacks found strength and encouragement to proceed down uncertain, and sometimes treacherous, roads to jobs and success in the 1930s. Although the Jim Crow era is gone, for the most part, the triangle of resources remains as vital now as it was then. Its viability will always be challenged by so-called progressive, but nontraditional, views, the destructive drug and substance abuse culture, wrongful education through popular song lyrics, and acknowledgement of God without submission to God.

Chapter 2: Early Days

My father, Jack Jeffrey McCowan, was called Robin by friends and family because unlike his siblings, he had reddish skin as a child. When I was a youngster, my aunts and uncles called him Robin, and I wondered why. At that point, I did not know much about my father. Since his siblings and cousins referred to him as Robin, I got used to it and thought it to be special. I'm not sure if he liked it, but it became permanent.

It's interesting that families and friends lovingly and otherwise attach descriptive titles to folks. As is often the case, a nickname nearly replaces the birth name.

Such labeling was used by Christ when he referred to two disciples, James and John, as the "sons of thunder." They were, no doubt, a lively pair, and as we're told in scripture, they had very high opinions of themselves as shown in their support of their mother's request that they sit on either side of Jesus on His throne.

Adam must also be given credit as one having a penchant for naming things. He was so good that God looked on with interest as Adam named all the animals. Whatever he called them became the official name. (Genesis 2:19) While his wife was formally named Eve, she was also called woman by Adam. However, truth be told, according to Genesis 2:23, Adam initially hailed her "This." "This" is not flattering and certainly not a name for a person, so we see the first, and typical, mindless response of a man to a beautiful woman. Let's give Adam a break; he had just awakened from a deep, anesthesia-like sleep. God brought him this strikingly beautiful woman. Moreover, he had never seen a woman, and she stood naked. In that situation, maybe "This" was appropriate.

The McCowan family lived in Karnack, TX, a town in northeastern Harrison County about three miles from the western Louisiana border, fourteen miles from Marshall,

28

and twenty-six miles from Shreveport. The town was named after the city of Karnack in ancient Egypt because of how the community was geographically aligned with the city of Port Caddo, Texas, relative to that of Karnack and Thebes in Egypt.

Karnack is and was a place replete with pine woods and mostly farm and timber land. According to my uncle Mack, the city had a jail, a post office, a midwife, and a store. The post office opened in 1898 when cotton and other commodities where shipped from Karnack.

While there was a jail, there was no police station or police service. The postman, Alan Moore, served as part time deputy. The story has been told how Mr. Moore, a white gentleman gave some local blacks a hard time and beat up a few. He was ultimately shot and killed by local folks in retribution, according to Uncle Mack, an example of small town justice. Anyone needing to go to court or a policeman had to travel to Marshall, TX, the birth place of George Forman, the eighth greatest boxer of all time and promoter of the George Forman Grill.

The town has remained small with a population of 100 in 1915 to subsequent growth to 850 by the early 1940s with twenty-two businesses in town.(1) Karnack received media attention from 1989 to 1991, when Pershing

29

missiles were destroyed in the Longhorn Army Ammunition Plant located there. The ammunition plant was established in 1942 to make TNT during WW II. My father's brother, Otis, worked there for a short time. In 1955, the plant came under direction of the Thiokol Corporation for the development of solid fuel rocket motors. The plant was officially deactivated in 1995. It exists today only as a wildlife preserve.

Today Karnack boasts the presence of an elementary and high school, a dentist, a doctor, a car dealership, six churches, Caddo Lake State Park, and several bed-and-breakfasts. Uncle Otis once made the comment that there was "nothing down there," referring to the part of town where they grew up. He was right.

The 1930 census listed my grandfather, Albert McCowan, as thirty-seven-years-old, and my grandmother, Bertha McCowan, as twenty-six-years-old. According to that record, they had four children: Addis (Uncle Spend) as eight, Bernice as six, Otis as three, and Wesley (Uncle Mac) as one. For whatever reason Aunt Ruby wasn't listed but she would have been four. At this time my father, the youngest, wasn't born yet.

In addition to names and ages of the family, the 1930 census questionnaire, a list of twenty-eight questions on a punch card, asked about the place of birth, high school or college education, the ability to read and write, and citizenship. Families were asked if they owned a radio! This was considered a luxury, and furthermore, the government was interested in the connectedness of the U.S. and the ability to reach a large number of people through this medium. Just think if we no longer had cell phones, text messaging, email, all the varieties of social media such as Twitter and its offshoots. Life would be hard; however, we wouldn't have spam, junk mail, and unsolicited and annoying, if not offensive, advertisements, pop ups, and other marketing ploys to deal with.

The acting director of the U.S. Census Bureau, Joseph A. Hill, thought the number of census questions was "close to the limit." After reaching a peak number of thirty-eight questions in 1940, the number declined.

In 2010, only ten questions were on the questionnaire. From these questions, the U.S. government decides on the distribution of approximately $400 billion dollars to cover the costs of schools, highways, public transportation, hospitals, libraries, police and fire protection, housing subsidies, job training, employment services, a variety of educational programs, and more. I suppose someone

31

showed up at the McCowan household in 1930 and asked my grandparents the census questions.

My grandfather, whom my father considered as his best friend, was listed in the census as a farmer; however, his primary occupation was a log cutter. He would leave for work on Sunday night and return Friday night. He was usually paid on Friday and brought money home for groceries. The shopping was done at Taylor's store in Karnack. Mr. Thomas Jefferson Taylor, the store owner, was the father of Claudia Taylor (Ladybird Johnson), the wife of Lyndon Johnson, the 36th President of the U.S.

Opening in 1912, the general store sold food supplies for people and animals. Clothing, shoes, and even two or three caskets were kept in the store. A customer could buy soda for five cents, a loaf of bread for seven cents, and gasoline for sixteen-to-seventeen cents a gallon. This store was stereotypical, having floor to ceiling shelves laden with wares for sale in every available inch of space. The store served as a meeting place for farmers and townspeople. A potbelly stove, a pickle barrel, and a checkerboard stood in a corner with a couple of chairs around it. A sign hung above the store that read, "T.J. Taylor–Dealer in Everything." And rightly so. A degree of nostalgia is attached to the general store even today as there is a general store museum located in Palm Springs, CA, called Ruddy's 1930s General Store Museum. According to their website, the museum is believed to be one of the largest displays of unused 1930s general store merchandise in the U.S.

Mr. Taylor was an important man. As my uncle Mack said, "He owned the town."

Among the local blacks, Mr. Taylor was known as "Mister Boss," but was known as "Cap'n Taylor" by his business associates. He became wealthy by using the profits from his store to loan money to farmers at a 10% interest and by investing heavily in real estate. He owned 15,000 acres of cotton.

Lady Bird Johnson said of her father, "He lived by his own rules."

Some of the bricks from the razed store were used to build the current post office, a small building at the town's main intersection.

My grandfather, Albert McCowan was born in 1893, in Batts, TX, a small community near Karnack. He died August 25, 1937, in a logging truck accident and was buried in the Batts cemetery. My grandfather, a tall, light-skinned, kind-hearted gentleman, spent some time making bootleg whiskey and trying a bit of it himself.

33

His father, Grandpa Newt (Newton), was a mulatto of Irish decent. His mother, Jane Williams, also known as Big Mama, was a Blackfoot Indian remembered for her long hair worn in two braids. The Blackfoot Indians are known to have their origins in Canada and Montana. I don't know Big Mama's roots. The American Indians in that area were of the Caddo Nation, which was comprised of the Natchitoches, Hasinai, and the Kadohadacho ethnic groups.

Although my grandfather was listed in the U.S census as a farmer, most of the farming was done by father's older brothers. They grew corn, peas, peanuts, and cotton. A portion of the corn was fed to their hogs, and the rest was used for family food. The cotton was taken to the town cotton gin, owned by W. H. Wurtzburger, and was sold for a meager profit.

The cotton gin, a machine that separated the cotton from its seeds, was invented by a Yale-educated inventor named Eli Whitney in 1793. The invention was thought to solidify slavery because of its marked efficiency in increasing the amount of cotton sent to market, an increase from around 500,000 pounds of cotton to market per year to about 93 million pounds. This marked increase called for greater numbers of slaves from West African countries to meet this demand. Not until 1863, seventy years following the invention of the cotton gin, did the Emancipation Proclamation officially free the slaves.

My grandmother, Bertha, was born in 1911, in Harrison County, TX, to Dave Tyler and Emma Irving. She died in March of 1946, at the young age of 35 from an infection.

My father's family lived on a farm in a small, plain, two-bedroom house. Early on they lived in a large home, built by my father's grandfather, but after Big Momma died in 1939 there was a forest fire that spread to the house and burned it down along with three nearby homes.

My grandmother had arranged for a laborer from the community to lay a concrete foundation for a new house. Two of my father's brothers, Otis, fifteen, and Mack, twelve, started the work on the new home. They chopped down the trees in the nearby forest. With the use of an axe, maul, and chisel, they fashioned planks for the frame of their new home. They had to do this work alone, having lost their father a few years before. According to Uncle Mack, his brother, Otis, did most of the work. I wonder how they knew how to build a house. Perhaps some local men gave instructions and dropped by for encouragement and assistance as the boys hammered nails and cut wood.

However, the storyline that Uncle Mack gave me goes differently. The boys had no major work experience, though they had worked with wood, making a dog house or two and some small play wagons. That's like going from grade school directly to college. Their older brother, Addis, had moved away. Their new home was larger than their first house, having four rooms: a bedroom for their mother, a living room, a back bedroom, and a kitchen. They covered the roof with shingles. Neither the outside nor the inside was painted because of a lack of money to buy the paint. There were no bricks to adorn the outside and no dry wall for the inside, but in the words of my uncle Mack, "It was a good house."

How can you possibly keep a house warm with no dry wall and insulation? It's hard to think of living in such a house, but I didn't live during that time or have the mind set of Uncle Mack or his siblings.

What made it a good house? My uncles were proud of the house and it was sufficient for their needs. Furthermore, they built the house with their sweat and might. It is amazing that two youngsters built a house for their family and then occupied the home. One can appreciate how responsible those two youngsters were, a responsibility spurred on by the local environment and economic situation.

There was no fence to surround their home, which sat in the middle of a verdant pasture. An unnamed dirt road, graded once or twice a year, passed in front of the house. No doubt a great place for kids to play, but not a great place for riding comfort.

A total of three houses were built on the property, the David Pilot estates, owned by my father's family. The girls slept in the living room. Consistent with the times and geographic location, the McCowan family house had no running water, no indoor toilets, no electricity, no gas, and no telephone. The family owned no automobile. Water had to be retrieved from a spring that ran through the community. This spring flowed year round and provided all their water needs, including fishing.

The boys rose early to chop wood—a daily chore—for heating purposes and for cooking. How many miles of jogging would that be equivalent to? How many cups of coffee would that morning activity replace?

House lamps containing kerosene were lit at dark. No scented kerosene then, just the classic vapors.

Evan Mills states that "typical kerosene lamps delivered between one and six lumens per square meter (lux) of useful light, compared to typical western standards of 300 lux for tasks such as reading." [1] Kerosene lighting during the 1930s was suboptimal for reading. Stan Jensen said these lamps "were so dim you almost had to use a flashlight to see if they were on,". No wonder my father always wanted more light in our Compton house. Most rooms in our house were very bright. Unusually bright!

The outhouse was an institution in itself. I'm grateful to the person who thought of bringing the outhouse inside the house and in a more acceptable, user-friendly version. It was nice to be out in nature and to hear the accompanying sounds, including the birds, cows, and horses, but on the other hand, the insects, lack of heat and light, the aroma, and the small space made the call of nature a cause to be delayed.

In the past, I had a few visits to one of these institutions. I'd heard stories of a scorpion or two, greeting a potential user, and I had feared falling through the oversized seat (or platform as it was more appropriately called) and never being seen again. The present day yard-throne remains underdeveloped and evokes a similar response. Okay. Movin' on!

My grandmother canned plums, peaches, blackberries, and other foods. I don't remember my father commenting on how good a cook his mother was. I presume she cooked well enough so there were no bad memories. My father told of occasionally not having food for breakfast and enduring his stomach growling at school.

As surmised, my grandmother made some clothes for the family and quilts. Are young girls taught to do these things anymore?

Store-bought toys were in the home only at Christmas and often consisted of an inexpensive cap pistol, a harmonica, and dolls for the girls or an inexpensive toy that didn't last long. Of course, at other times, my father and his siblings made toys from whatever was available. It's been said that the best thing a child can do with a toy is break it, and the next best thing is to make it. Two scenarios making room for creativity and exercise of the mind.

The family attended the Friendship Baptist Church. My grandparents were members. My grandmother was not an usher, and my grandfather was not a deacon. The original Friendship Church burned down and later was rebuilt. The new version stands today.

As with many black families of that time and beyond, church played a vital role in the socialization, political machination, education, and spiritual growth of the local community. The black barbershop and beauty parlor have been similar bastions of community support. On a lighter side, in Craig Marberry's book *Cuttin' Up: Wit and Wisdom from Black Barber Shops*, Reginald Attucks, a barber, states that "the cop's gonna come. The preacher's gonna come. The gangsta's gonna come. The barber shop's the one place where you can put all the wrong people at the same time. It's the final black frontier."

The McCowan's had a few hogs, cows, and horses. The hogs and cows provided food. These animals added to the daily chores. The cows provided sweet milk, which then clabbered and then was churned for fifteen-to-twenty minutes into butter and buttermilk. The family did not have a refrigerator but an icebox, also called a Coolerator, in which twenty-five pounds of ice was packed. Items contained in the icebox, remained cool for about a week. The meat from the farm animals was kept in a smoke house or was salted to preserve it.

My father attended Buck Ridge Elementary School. While his brothers graduated from a local high school in Karnack, he graduated from Phyllis Wheatly High School in Houston in 1949. This school, started in 1927, has graduated notables such as the late Congresswoman Barbara Jordan and the late Congressman Mickey Leland, both from Texas. The school was segregated since the Brown v. Board of Education decision was not determined until 1954.

Aunt Ruby said that my father was very smart and read well at four years. She said local people thought he was a genius. On the other hand, my uncle Mack said he was spoiled and considered a mama's boy. I find it hard to believe the latter opinion, but my father's siblings would know. According to Aunt Ruby, he was constantly reading books, a memory I shared, but the mama's boy picture didn't fit, in my opinion. My father didn't act like a mama's boy. He apparently grew out of that phase. He seemed tough and had his way of doing things.

My aunt Bernice told the story of her carrying my father in a pail down the road. My father was four or five at the time. She set the pail on the road while she went to get something. A big cow came along, and my father stood in the pail and balled his fists to hit the cow.

41

Generally, a child that age would run out of the pail, yelling rather than standing to fight the big animal. And in my experiences I never saw my father shaking in his boots and for years thought nothing scared him.

He was good at hiding his feelings. People said my father looked serious. This might be described as a cool pose. Richard Majors, who wrote the book, *Cool Pose,* describes it as a mask to hide deeper vulnerabilities and something that black males (and others) use to make sense of their everyday lives. The former rationale for cool pose is probably generally more applicable and often an effective deterrent to unsolicited questions and encounters with others, the usual desired outcome of "cool pose."

My father's brothers didn't want to take him with them because he would wander off, chase butterflies, get into mischief, and wouldn't do what they asked him to do. Sounds like the stereotypical little brother-big brother relationship. He got on their nerves, but they looked out for him because he was their brother. They didn't throw him in a pit and sell him to passing Ishmaelites!

My father was five when his father died in a logging truck accident. At that age your opinion about the death hovers around the thought that your father, whom you considered your best friend, left you, and maybe it was your fault. Perhaps he often looked down the road to see if his daddy was coming or searched the house and property for him, and listened for his voice. The large, gaping, pain-saturated hole in the heart eventually recedes into a noticeable scar that occasionally bleeds.

After my grandfather died, my grandmother married Warren Neal in 1945 and moved from Karnack. My father, 15, stayed with his brother, Mack. No father and then his mother leaves. Frustrations and confusion for a growing young man. Alienation, guilt, fear, and uncertainty can subsequently distort a person's thinking and social relationships if the aftermath of abandonment is not dealt with early on. Uncle Mack said he had to get my father out of fist fights at school frequently. No Daddy at five and Mom leaves at fifteen; gotta grow up fast, want to or not!

Today, the school counselor, minister, psychiatrist, and any other trained individual might be sought to counsel a child. There are programs to help children deal with the pain of death, divorce, separation, or abandonment.

What happens to that pain if it's not addressed? Outside of his teenage fisticuffs, I don't know how my father dealt with his anger. He did not take criticism well, and he didn't socialize. After an occasional talk with neighbors, he often came home angry and stated that so-and-so was "crazy." However, he didn't rant and rave about these injured relationships. On the upside, it was fun to find out who in the neighborhood was crazy!

My father was on the track team in high school. My Uncles, Mack and Otis, were on the team too. My father used to boast that he had run the 100 yard dash in 9.5 seconds, which was fast for that race. He later retracted this claim and stated he ran close to it. Close is relative. Maybe it was 9.8 seconds, but then maybe it was 11.5 seconds, which ain't too good. Just hearing about it was the treat; it didn't matter to me how fast he ran it. He gave another view of himself, one which I had not anticipated. That was nice. I never asked if he had won any races or whether he was the fastest runner in his high school class. I was satisfied with what I had learned, and there was no reason to deflate the serendipity with further questioning.

Bibliography

1. Evan, Mills "Technical and Economic Performance Analysis of Kerosene Lamps

and Alternative Approaches to Illumination in Developing Countries"

June 28, 2003 Lawrence Berkeley National Laboratory.

Chapter 3 A Place called Karnack

On June 8, 2011, my wife and I went to Marshall, TX, to help Uncle Mack appeal an almost tripled property tax increase on the David Pilot Estates. Uncle Mack, his wife Unita, and their daughter, Vercia, came to Marshall from Los Angeles. We left Charleston, WV, Tuesday evening, June 7, and flew to Shreveport, Louisiana, rented a car, and drove forty-five minutes to Marshall.

Marshall is a pleasant northeastern town of 24,000 population. It's known as the Cultural Capitol of East Texas and the birthplace of Boogie Woogie music. Four colleges are established there. One is Wiley College, an historically black institution.

The following morning we drove thirteen miles west on highway 43 to Karnack. There wasn't much to the city. The center of town is located at an intersection and is comprised of a post office, a community center, a church, and a city utility office. No traffic light hangs at this intersection because of little traffic. In fact, we saw no cars parked at the buildings. It was eerie!

We traveled the roads that led from the central intersection and took pictures of deer, interesting homes and buildings, and a variety of vegetation. We ventured farther and deeper into the rural settings, not knowing where we were going; so we decided to return later with Uncle Mack as our guide.

Later that day, Vercia made an excellent presentation to the tax board and provided documents that proved the taxes were too high. It was a treat to see how well-organized she was.

The board was comprised of Karnack citizens. We sat on one side of the room while two tax officials sat on the other. The officials had lowered the taxes once, but according to Vercia's calculations, they should have been lowered more. The board did not agree. We left the tax office disappointed and without recourse.

We returned to Karnack that afternoon. Uncle Mack said he had been there the prior day, and several men in company trucks ushered them off the property. A host of deer flies also did their share in ushering them off the property.

We went there by route 1793 to Peters Chapel Road; we turned right and traveled a partially paved and then dirt road bordered on both sides by a dense forest of verdant trees at least forty feet high. A rare house was seen along the way.

After a mile, we reached Buckhorn Road, a dirt road that was there when Uncle Mack was a boy. This road led to their house. No more pavement, only red dirt, rocks, and bumps.

No street lights lined the road, so I was glad we had started early not to encounter night. Uncle Mack commented that the night would get so dark, you could barely see your hand in front of you.

An occasional huge deer fly hurled itself onto the windshield of our rented Subaru SUV as we drove along. These blood-sucking flies can bite your skin with their razor-sharp jaws until you bleed. They are attracted by movement and dark clothes. They can function as a vector for Lyme's disease, anthrax, and several other diseases. Luckily we were not bitten.

The tree growth overhead blocked the sun so the day's light grew darker as we moved farther from civilization. We traveled another mile before we came to the property. What Uncle Mack had known as flat farm land, the old Friendship Community, was completely covered and lost within a forest.

As we drove along, Uncle Mack pointed to a place where a house stood that he and his family had rented for $5 a month while they built their new home. He pointed out an area where a natural spring had been and noted how good the water had tasted.

As he reminisced, he told us how his father would take the family to Marshall in the family wagon. They left about 6 a.m. and traveled four hours down the unpaved, uneven, and unforgiving dirt road. That amount of time in a wagon with no rubber tires, shock absorbers, or off-road advantages of an independent suspension, must have been a memorable ride with subsequent lingering stiffness, aching joints, and a stubborn reluctance to ride again in the near future. On the other hand, the lack of options demands a compromise of accepting the bad and hoping for better options in the future. These memories I'm sure were quite influential in leading my father and his sibling to decide to move and not return to Karnack.

When arriving at Marshall, my father and his siblings shopped, and perhaps took in a movie, and then returned home around midnight via the wagon and road ordeal. Uncle Mack laughed as he recalled that his parents purchased his and his siblings' shoes for $1.98. They were made of a cardboard-type material. He said when the shoes got wet, the sole's front part separated from the rest of the shoe and flapped when they walked. Once he cut the flapping part off, and got fussed at by his mother. Being skillful she took wire and sewed the sole back on the shoe.

Artist Mike Leavitt has made numerous cardboard shoes and displayed them in art shows such as the Cardboard Shoe Show of New York City.

I don't think anyone actually wears this type of shoe today.....uh, I take that back.

From Karnack to Compton:

Buckhorn Rd is the "street" to my father's birthplace.

T. J. Taylor Mansion

My mother's parents - Lonnie and Carrie Hawkins, Texarkana, Tx

My mother's brothers. From left- James, Virgil, Warren, Kenneth (in back), Lonnie, Ben, and Bob.

From Karnack to Compton:

My mother and her sisters. From left - Joyce, Margie, Doris, Ethel, Verline, Barbara (Mom), and Hazel

My sister Ange and I circa 1960, Compton, CA

Daddy and Uncle Otis, 1950s.

Daddy's Parents, Albert and Bertha McCowan

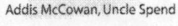

Addis McCowan, Uncle Spend

Daddy in his 20s

Chapter 4 The Compton Years

My father joined the U.S. Army in 1950 and received an honorable discharge in 1953. He was in the army during the Korean conflict, but he didn't go to war. I assume the military valued his educational pursuits and interest in electronics more than his ability to occupy the battle front. I saw an old picture of him in his uniform. He was probably nineteen, but looked younger; his facial expression seemed to ask, *What am I doing here?*

He told us his commanding officer had him dig ditches and then fill them in. There were other meaningless tasks, as he described them. He didn't talk about the military in a positive light. While the military had been desegregated in 1948 by President Truman's Executive Order 9981, institutionalized racism (military Jim Crowism) persisted as the majority of blacks worked in the mess halls, as duty soldiers, and drivers. Rank and promotion were hard to achieve.

My father was not a military man and sought to express his patriotism in another way. His experiences in the Jim Crow era and military motivated him to go through our Compton neighborhood to register people to vote, thus exercising their power be heard through this right.

After leaving the Army, my father traveled to South Central Los Angeles in 1953 to live with his older brother, Spend. My father bought a light-green, 1951, Pontiac Chieftain. This vehicle had a radio, a tissue dispenser, and under-seat heating. Engine power was rated at 90 or 106 hp, depending on if it was a six or eight-cylinder model. No power brakes or air conditioning came with the car. It cost him around $1,985, a gallon of regular gas cost twenty-seven cents, and he got between fifteen and twenty-four miles per gallon for gas mileage, depending how he drove. I would say my father got closer to fifteen mpg! The gas pedal could get a workout. He was proud of that car. While I wasn't around to see the car, I'm sure Dad washed and kept it tuned up. No Armor All to keep the tires shiny and black then. This product hit the market in 1966.

My father and mother met in Los Angeles about September 1953. My mother was living with her aunt Cat, my maternal grandfather's sister, on 73rd St. in South Central Los Angeles. My father lived next door with his brother, Spend.

My mother, Barbara Ruth Hawkins, was born in Ashdown, AR, to Lonnie and Carrie Hawkins. She is the third of seventeen (yes, 17!) children. Her father was born in Ashdown in 1909 and was the oldest of four children born to Benjamin and Francis Hawkins. Benjamin, one of seven children, was born in 1875 to Burrel Hawkins, who was born in 1830 to James Alexander Hawkins, a gentleman born in Africa, possibly Ghana in 1811, and brought to the U.S. as a slave.

His slave master was named Benjamin F. Hawkins and there we have the origin of the Hawkins name. Perhaps his true name had been Kojo, Kwame, Kofi, or Kwesi in following a popular Ghana tradition of naming a child after the week day of the child's birth. Perhaps he was from the Ashanti, Fanti, or Akan tribes and was destined to be and dreamed of becoming a great leader. He was probably tall and strong and could run fast. He was most likely a fearless hunter, but was kind, respectful, and chose his words carefully. Then he was caught by slave traders and chained to other unfortunate Africans in the malodorous bowels of a slave ship, carried through the infamous middle passage with a final destination being the antebellum southern U.S. So the story went for many of that era, living on the west coast of Africa.

My mother stated my father often sat on the brick fence where he lived and talked to her. After a courtship, my mother and father married March 27, 1954. I was born into the household a year later. They lived in an apartment in South Central LA for two years.

We moved to Compton, CA, in 1957, the year my sister, Angela, was born. It was a pleasant, quiet community, sandwiched between South Central LA, Gardena, Carson, and Lynwood. The city, incorporated in 1889, is named after Griffith D. Compton, who had donated the land. A portion of the land, known as Richland Farms, was reserved for agricultural use. The farming opportunity attracted blacks in the 1950s.

Compton remained a primarily white community until the 1970s. Most of the businesses in downtown Compton were owned by whites. About twenty-five to thirty stores, including J.C.Penney, J. J. Newberry's, Woolworth's, and other businesses, like Bank of America, Security Pacific Bank, several jewelry stores, furniture stores, an abandoned movie theater called the Compton, and the post office, crammed into a two-block area. One could buy almost everything he needed, except a car. Even a grocery store was located on a side street. The feared material store, one of my mother's favorite spots, was located at the corner of Compton Blvd. and Alameda St. It was filled with bundles of colorful fabrics. There was barely enough room to walk in the store. My mother would not leave despite my sister's and my pleading.

Up until the 1960s, one could catch the Pacific Electric Railway Red Car on Willowbrook Ave. and ride twenty miles between Long Beach and downtown Los Angeles. There are few remnants of this downtown Compton as most of the buildings were demolished in the 1970s.

As a kid, I thought it was strange that on any given day horseback riders, as we called them, trotted along 156th St., where our house was located, leaving their trail while airplanes from the nearby Compton Airport occupied the air. This airport had opened in the 1920s. The neighborhood kids got a kick out of watching the different aircraft, planes, and choppers that flew overhead.

The runway was located a block from our street. Such proximity had its risks with an occasional airplane crash. An airplane crashed into the Mobil station at the corner of Alondra and Central Ave., and several crashed into neighborhood homes. The sound of one of these crafts stalling, as they often did, sent all eyes upward and prepared legs to run.

We attempted to go onto the airport property from time to time to see the aircraft. High fences and barbwire were subsequently erected.

While we thought the place was unique, that opinion was not shared by some using the airport. One blogger had this to say recently, "This airport is GHETTOOOOOOO !!!!! LOL One of the few uncontrolled airports in the LA terminal area. I've only been there once to practice my uncontrolled airport radio calls. The two little runways are so cute...but that's the opposite of ideal from a pilot's POV. It felt barely wide enough for my main gear, and even though I landed super slow, I still had to slam on the brakes to avoid running off the end. lol We taxied past the old broken planes with flat tires. They just looked SAD and reminded me of broken-down cars on cinder blocks in people's front yards! Pretty much what you'd expect at COMPTON airport. lol" After all these years, the facility looks well-maintained and is used often. So back off, dude!

Until recently, blacks made up over 90% of Compton's population. Currently, Latinos make up the majority (56.8%) of the city's 93,692 occupants while blacks comprise 40.3%, according to the 2000 U.S. Census. [1]

In November 2010, Compton was rated number eight on a list of the most dangerous cities in America. Additionally, Neighborhood Scout notes the crime rate per square mile in Compton was 402 while it was 147 for the state of California and 49.6 for the nation. [2]

The high rate of crime has been attributed to gangs and drugs. The influence of gangsta rap, in particular by N.W.A (with Compton's Dr. Dre, Easy-E, and Ice Cube) in their album *Straight Outta Compton* in 1988) can't be ignored. *When I'm called off, I got a sawed off, squeeze the trigger, and bodies are hauled off.* In terms of influence, 3 million copies of the album were sold, placing the recording in a double platinum category. Violence against women and police and other crimes were promoted in the lyrics. It's ironic that whenever I visit friends and family there, I never see evidence that life is as bad in Compton as the media says. As the saying goes, *if you look for trouble, you will find it.*

61

Other notable folk that have resided in Compton at some time include former President George W. Bush, former Dodger Duke Snider, actor James Coburn, meteorologist Al Roker, comedienne Niecy Nash, and Venus and Serena Williams.

Our neighborhood was not quiet. Between the boom boxes, police sirens, barking dogs, the morning rooster, occasional yelling neighbors, airplanes, and news, recreational, and police helicopters, there were few moments of absolute silence.   And excessively loud motorcycles were driven up and down the street at times.

People can become accustomed to the sounds over time, and their absence is notable and foreign. A transition to a peaceful, quiet environment may ironically create longing for noise and chaos to feel at home. My close friends and I experienced this at one time or another in the distant past. Despite the traffic, other neighborhood kids and I played baseball and football in the street. It's amazing that we didn't get hit by a car or that our parents let us play in the street.

My father kept the front and back yards of our Compton home immaculate. It was his hobby. We had various tropical plants in the front yard: rhododendrons, yucca plants, dichondra grass, etc. He spent hours at yard

62

work, digging, weeding, and planting flowers. He placed a good-sized ornament that looked like a miniature mountain in the front. It had a functioning waterfall. He installed a sprinkler system with five strategically placed sprinkler heads to water the entire yard. No one else on our street had such a system. I'm sure this work was rewarding to him in more than one way.

Man's first home was in a garden. After disobeying, an act that changed him and his relationship with the Creator, continued work with agriculture was required as therapy. So therapeutic gardening has deep roots. Genesis 3:17 says, "Cursed is the ground *for thy sake,*" and in verse 23, "*the Lord God sent him forth from the garden of Eden, to till the ground from whence he was taken.*"

Here is an interesting quote: "Working in the garden, gathering flowers and fruit, listening to the birds praising God, the patients will be wonderfully blessed. Angels of God will draw near to them. They will forget their sorrows. Melancholy and depression will leave them. The fresh air and sunshine and the exercise taken will bring them life and vitality. The wearied brain and nerves will find relief." [2] The soothing and therapeutic benefits of this physical activity is known by many, but yet underutilized.

Daddy told us we couldn't play in the front yard. Of course, we did, anyway, when he wasn't home. The yard's shape made it a great place to play baseball. He would have had a heart attack if he had seen us running on his nicely kept, green grass.

My father's artistic flair, attention to detail, and desire to represent himself and his family positively were seen in the care of the yard. It can be said that close inspection of a man's yard may provide a view of what type of man he is and the desires of his heart.

The back yard did not fare as well as the front; nevertheless, it was usually well kept. We had fruit trees, including terrible tasting plums, watery peaches, loquats, which are a bizarre tropical fruit that is watery, tangy, and slightly sweet to the taste, a barren lemon tree, and a banana tree that occasionally grew a tiny banana. Such a stark contrast to the richness of the front yard! The backyard seemed cursed. How could the fruit trees be so afflicted? A man's backyard may be a reflection of his worries and woes. I didn't help the situation since I threw rubber balls against the backyard fence and run all around to practice my baseball fielding skills.

My father owned a set of plant encyclopedias, which he studied often. This hobby of my father's provided him
64

with a great sense of satisfaction and accomplishment. It was also an outgrowth of his upbringing and seeing his brothers work in the fields.

My father put chlordane—a pesticide—around and under the house so we had no bugs for years. He would find old cloths and a flashlight and crawl under the house. Sometime later he would resurface covered with dirt and dust from head to toe. The Orkin Company was around then, but my father was a strong believer in doing tasks himself and saving a few dollars. Chlordane was banned in 1988 due to an increased risk for cancer of the breast, prostate, and brain, and leukemia, and lymphoma. Perhaps my father's developing cancer later in his life was related to this exposure.

My father had a few guns at home like most people in our neighborhood. He had a couple of pistols and a 410 gauge shotgun. I grew up thinking guns were used for protection and not for hunting. What did one hunt in Compton? The guns were for burglars or anyone breaking into our home.

My father shot a gun on New Year's Eve. He pointed the gun to the sky, and then we heard the loud, sharp pops as he fired a few rounds.

What goes up must come down, but where? A high school classmate's father was killed by a stray bullet.

New Year's Eve was an interesting time to listen for the different gun blasts. An occasional automatic weapon was heard, even a machine gun. Sometimes a huge bang made us wonder if someone had a bazooka. Why did someone need such weapons?

I never asked my father to let me shoot a gun. I had no interest in them. The thought of shooting another person was dreadful. I don't remember him going to a shooting range, probably because he was an experienced military man. However, I came to believe having a gun in the house probably wasn't a bad idea, especially after our house was broken into twice. A lawnmower was stolen from the garage. Three car stereos were stolen from the front of our house. On the other hand, the specter of a child finding and playing with a loaded gun in the home was a concern. Ok, don't load the gun and hide the ammo! Then when the burglar comes, someone asks, "Honey, where did I put the bullets?" So the hand gun debate continues.

I only shot a gun as a teenager and with my mother's brother Kenneth. We shot birds with a rifle with some big buckshot. I didn't feel good after shooting the birds. I wouldn't make a good hunter.

From time to time, a dog inhabited the back yard. Our first dogs when we were kids were named Queenie and Butch, common dog names in that part of town. Queenie got hit by a car. There weren't any leash laws. Butch spent his time trying to jump over the backyard gate. He finally figured how, but suffered significant scrapes to his abdomen, which led to his demise. We had a Doberman that was nervous and unpredictable. The most memorable dog was a Weimaraner named Chris. I had never seen a dog like her prior to having her as a pet. Green eyes and tan coat. Most neighborhood dogs were All-American, combinations of several breeds and looking like none, ones my father fondly referred to as *mutts*.

My father would usually prepare breakfast for my sister and I before school. My mother would come home from her night shift around 7:30 AM and go straight to bed. He would usually make pancakes. These were special pancakes which were about an inch thick. Each one would take up so much syrup that it was hard to detect the sweetness. We learned to pour the syrup on the side of the plate and quickly dab a piece of pancake onto the syrup before it started soaking it up. You could only eat a couple of these high volume pancakes.

On other days, he cooked his special brand of oatmeal. My sister said it was so thick that if we threw it against the wall, the oatmeal would stick. We thinned it with milk and added butter and sugar. Despite its thickness, it tasted good.

My father never complained about having to cook breakfast for us, and it never appeared to bother him. He never talked while he cooked or while we ate, but a sermon was preached in that verbal silence. Do your job faithfully, and don't complain. We never left for school hungry, because he never took a day off from being a father.

He baked cakes and special dishes occasionally. He baked a cake that cracked down the middle. Yeah! It was the St. Andreas Fault right down the middle of it. After he carefully frosted it, we still saw the fault line that suggested an earthquake had actually occurred inside the cake. I wonder what its ingredients were. My parents had a good laugh about it, and the cake didn't last long because it tasted really good. About that time, we began to refer to him as Chef Jeff. He occasionally made a peanut loaf that was very good, too.

He became serious about his cooking venture. He wore his apron and worked his magic. All his dishes were tasty. He made good vegetarian dishes.

Walking on the neighborhood fence tops was such fun. A network of red brick fences ran along the yards. The flat bricks were wide enough for a child to walk easily. My friends and I walked these fences and passed through six or seven backyards, ending around the corner. Some yards had a ferocious dog that jumped up the fence to bite us, so we carried stones to discourage the dogs.

Some yards contained fruit trees that we unlawfully visited. One elderly lady had fourteen peaches on a tree. We took all of them. She promptly called and told our parents. Such behavior ruined a parent's reputation as a model parent.

My father told us to stay off the fences. We were compliant as long as he was not at home, but not wearing watches, we stayed on the fences too long and found him waiting in the backyard with his crossed arms and a stern look.

"I thought I told you to stay off the fences more than once! Okay. You can't go outside to play for a month!" he told me.

Ouch! I remember trying to "play" with my friends while I sat in the front door's threshold while my friends played on our front porch or in our front yard. I found disobedience to be costly.

We attended the New Life Baptist Church. We drove the long distance from Compton into deep north Los Angeles. We took Central Ave. or Avalon Blvd. These streets were representative of the basic street layout of Los Angeles. One of the great things about Los Angeles is that one can take these north and south streets and travel many miles from Carson, or Long Beach, all the way to downtown Los Angeles. Or take numerous streets that run east and west and travel from city to city.

For our family, Central Ave. was the hub street, literally central to many of our travels. It was the primary route to grade school, church, and downtown Compton. The farther we drove on this street, the more fascinating it became. Interesting houses, people, numerous businesses, parks, fast food outlets, and too many traffic lights ran along this avenue.

The Black Muslim men sold their bean pies on corners. They dressed in their Sunday best with a thin bow tie neatly stuck to their heavily starched and whiter-than-white shirts in the heat of the day. The pies were a fund-raising effort by the Nation of Islam and encouraged by the late Elijah Mohammed.

"Bean pies! Bean pies! My brother, don't you want this bean pie?" they called.

The pies were individually packaged in a tidy pink box. We occasionally purchased one. They were tasty. We felt as though we had eaten healthy food.

An article in the June 12, 2011, *LA Times* newspaper told about Brian Mohammed, forty-two and a Nation of Islam member, who still sells bean pies for $7 each on a busy street corner in Los Angeles. The tradition lives on.

People wore colorful clothing along Central Ave. The man in his canary-yellow suit, pimping, as we said, was one of my favorites. With all I had seen, he was in the top three for interesting clothes. On the other end of the spectrum was the man walking down the street with no clothes on and a second man chasing him with a handful of clothes, yelling, "Hey! Put some clothes on, your black @%$$!"

My eyes were wide open for new sights on drives to church.

We sometimes passed the old Goodyear Tire Company while driving through South Central LA to see Uncle Glen, Aunt Cat, or to go to church. The company was located between Florence and Gage Streets. The large, red-brick, main building on the Goodyear site appeared stately and like a university in its form and central location. A tower on the roof contained a large clock seen from the surrounding streets. The institution-of-higher-learning feel of the building was retained in later years after it had been abandoned, even with its numerous broken windows.

A couple of big hangers housed the Goodyear blimp. Being interested in technical things, my father pointed these out to me. Once I saw the huge silver behemoth land as we passed in our car. For its enormous size, it was quiet and eerie. This was an ancestor to the blue-yellow-and-silver versions seen gracing the skies today. The Goodyear Tire Company closed the facility in 1977. It was torn down in the 1980s. One blimp is now kept in Carson, CA.

We attended the New Life Baptist Church because Aunt Cat, my mother's aunt, attended. She was my maternal grandfather's sister. My mother and father sang in the choir, although my father was the one who could actually sing, according to my mother. My sister Angela and I had godparents in that church, and the pastor's son was my best friend.

72

Church services were an interesting but sometimes unpleasant experience. I was afraid when some woman "got the spirit" and started shouting. None of the church men "got the spirit," as they called it. I wondered why. Sometimes the deacons had to escort a sister from the church with her arms and legs flailing because the spirit was "strong and long." No disrespect on worship styles is intended. This was the way church service appeared to me then.

I loved the church music. The pianist played with a good beat and rhythm. It seemed like a drummer and bass player wouldn't have added much.

Pastor Ross in his black robe sat in the pulpit. When it came time for him to preach, he rose slowly and spoke softly and slowly built his sermon with intensity and volume. Although I hadn't understood all that was said, I noticed the adults listened intently, so I tried to do the same. As much as a child's mind allowed anyway. The sermon continued forever, and at some point, he preached in a loud, rhythmic, sing-song voice.

The congregation responded with timed *amens*, humming, and shouts. The pianist chimed in with a few chords to enhance the experience. I was unsure what it all meant. I knew it represented the hot level on the intensity

73

dial. It was like jazz: improvised, rhythmic, cool, but not always understood.

After the sermon, someone, often the pastor, started singing a capella. The congregation joined in this deeply emotional song. Though I don't remember the words, I believe it was a crying out for God's help. The service ended soon.

A potluck dinner sometimes followed in the basement fellowship hall. The food was always delicious. Then came the long drive home.

Each Sunday this worship style was repeated, not just at New Life Baptist Church, but in many black churches across the continent. This time period was the early 1960s and this church experience was my introduction to black church culture.

We became Seventh-day Adventists (SDA) in 1965 through friends' influence and the church school my sister and I attended: the Los Angeles Union SDA School. My father did not become SDA. That was sad because we never worshipped as a family after that. The truth of the biblical Seventh-day Sabbath was compelling to us. And as it says in God's word: *There remaineth therefore a rest to the people of God. For he that is entered into his rest, he also hath ceased from his own works, as God did from his.* (Hebrews 4:9, 10)

Fourth of July celebrations were really fun. My father was the chief pyro-technologist and master of ceremonies, and he put on a good show. My sister and I enjoyed it. He bought Black Cat fireworks at the stand in the Avalon and Central parking lot. He purchased a small pack of fireworks that contained snakes that burned right out of the concrete when they were lit, Piccolo Petes that emitted piercing screams, colorful showering cones, and the traditional sparklers.

Once the fireworks were used, he'd buy more. But no firecrackers for his kids. My mother allowed us only to watch from the living room window. We were fine with this for a couple years.

My father owned a Harley Davidson motorcycle. I didn't see him ride it. I saw an old picture of him dressed in his big helmet and black leather riding jacket. He stood next to his Harley, parked in front of our house. I don't know what model the motorcycle was; it was good-sized and had to predate 1965.

He never owned another motorcycle and never expressed a desire to buy another. No doubt he reminisced from time to time about how it felt to ride in the wind or to rev up the engine or to zoom through traffic with ease.

In their article on *Famous Men and Their Motorcycles*, Brett and Kate McKay wrote, "Motorcycles represent a peculiar combination of several manly elements: danger, speed, singular focus, solitude, mechanics, noise, and physical skill." In brief, that means a hefty jolt of testosterone. Then cometh kids, bills, taxes, spousal advice, and...goodbye, motorcycle. With discipline, men send away their toys, but endogenous testosterone nags and searches for another vehicle of expression. And so...

He liked fast cars. He bought a 1955, pastel-blue-and-white Chevy coupe. It had a V8 engine and an old hydromatic transmission that roared when you gave it the gas, making the car sound souped up. The testosterone was talking.

He drove it for several years and then bought a blue, 1967 Camaro. That was the first year GM made the Camaro. The original engine in my father's car was a 210 hp, 327 cu in. He rebuilt the engine himself years later and installed a high performance camshaft and a four-barrel carburetor. As expected, the car was significantly faster. Even later, he bought a used truck with a rebuilt engine that was souped up.

He took my friends and me to Lyon's Drag Strip in Long Beach. As kids, we had so much fun watching the cars do burn outs and then take off, doing a wheel stand. The noise was incredibly loud. We could hear the race cars from our house on Saturday nights.

In the mid-to-late '60s, my father was adamant about controlling what we kids watched on television. He was convinced TV was a source of many evils and intellectual demise. Consequently, he marked the programs in the TV guide my sister and I could watch. He picked documentaries and other educational programs. It was a television diet; whatever we didn't like was "good for us." He gave us a break with a few cartoons and sitcoms. Most programs we wanted to watch were not circled by his red felt pen.

This was tough at first because at school, our classmates talked enthusiastically about TV shows, and we hadn't seen them.

Our father softened after we'd lobbied for rights to watch certain shows. He had made his point of helping us understand we needed discipline and discrimination on what we watched and the amount of time we spent in front of the idiot box, as he called it.

In his book, *Remote Controlled*, Joe Wheeler has a cartoon of Adam and Eve in the Garden of Eden, looking into the Tree of the Knowledge of Good and Evil, where the serpent offers them a television. That's a powerful message. User, beware! Rather, don't use it all.

My father made my sister and me work math problems from a book in the summers. We had to complete a couple of pages' worth before playing. This went on for four-to-five years of our elementary school time. He tried to give his kids an advantage in a world where expectations were not high and too many doors remained closed. Today websites will solve math problems for you! Is that good?

Our parents made us take piano lessons from an enthusiastic piano teacher in Compton on Tuesday nights in a small, dimly lit room next to her garage. Having practiced insufficiently made Tuesday evenings painful. Practicing insufficiently was the norm for my sister and me. We waited nervously as the preceding student finished his lesson.

The best part was thumbing through one of the *National Geographic* magazines in her large collection. What a relief!

On occasion the teacher rose in frustration to show us how the beautiful song should be played. She made the song sound nice and sometimes sang the lyrics while playing. She tilted her head back, increased her vocal volume, and then turned on the vibrato. Quite impressive. While this was a treat, it was also a confirmation I didn't have what it took to be a pianist or a singer. And, were we playing from the same music book?

My father tried to make us practice daily. He made me wrist splints so I kept my wrists straight while playing the piano. He returned from work and, as was his custom, asked us if we had practiced the piano and done our homework. We couldn't play unless those had been finished. What a pain to sit at that piano for those long thirty minutes.

The piano was not my instrument or my sister's although she had memorized Beethoven's "Für Elise" and played it often, assuring our parents that the money and time spent on piano lessons was not wasted. We have to consider that just because a kid can't play the piano after numerous lessons; it does not mean the lessons were a waste of time. The exposure to songs, harmony, rhythm, and music theory was priceless.

As adults, we must recognize that what we wished we had accomplished we sometimes force upon our children to live our dreams vicariously. My father sometimes sat and played a simple piano song. His big fingers plunked the keys, and he tried not to watch his hands as he read the page, counted aloud, and kept his wrists straight. The treat was to see him sit on that blasted piano bench like us. I would love to see him do that again.

One day my father took my friend and me to fly my kite. The place was the oversized, sandy playfield at Charles Bursch Elementary School, a block from our house. The neighborhood kids attended the school for kindergarten. I had purchased the red paper kite at the drug store for fifteen cents. What joy there was in looking through the kite box for just the right one! We placed a tail of old rags and of ample length.

Do people fly kites like this anymore? Now people talk about kite-sailing, kite-surfing, kite-skiing, kite-boogying, and whatever else one can attach a kite to for locomotion. If you attended a kite festival, you might see multi-colored inflatable kites, parafoils, deltas, rokkakus, cellulars, sleds, diamonds, novelty kites, and more. Folks would talk kite-speak. You'd find famous kite flyers, exhibits, and food.

My kite was a diamond. Only two types were available at the drug store; the diamond and the box kites. They were all paper with wood support sticks but none were multicolored. My father flew it with plenty of string. He demonstrated the correct way to get the kite airborne: tossing the kite in the air to catch wind and then running until it took flight.

The kite went up, up, and far away. It appeared like it was five or six blocks away. I was amazed at the distance. The fact that it stayed in one spot in the air and my father just stood, holding the string with the greatest of ease, made me jump with crazed excitement. How simple, inexpensive, and yet deeply rich and everlasting. Every kid should have a red kite.

My father graduated from West Coast University in Los Angeles in 1969 with a Bachelor of Science degree in electronic engineering.

His graduation day and mine were scheduled the same day. My father decided only to attend my eighth grade graduation. He never said a word about it to me, and so I knew nothing about this until years later. This spoke of his self-sacrificing nature and his humility. He worked harder than I did for a diploma, holding down a full-time job, being a father, and going to school simultaneously.

81

I would have liked to have seen him dressed in a graduation robe and hat. No pictures were taken to commemorate his academic efforts. No one thought to memorialize his monumental feat overcoming poverty, escaping a childhood, for the most part, without parents, being victorious in a Jim Crow society, and being one of a handful of blacks in his field. On this latter part, he stated he was usually the only black doing whatever job in space-technology areas.

Poet Milica Franchi De Luri wrote:

"Silence speaks

Silence screams

Silence talks louder than any word

that cuts true the heart like a sword."

In his journey to achieve his degree, my father attended classes at University of California Los Angeles (UCLA) and worked as a technician at the Space Technology Laboratories (STL) until he graduated. He was then elevated to engineer status.

Chapter 5 Hunene!

My father's story would be incomplete without mention of my mother's story. He would not have been the Jack McCowan I knew without her.

My mother was born in Ashdown, AR, in 1934, and like my father, was delivered by a midwife. However, the midwife was her maternal grandmother, whom the family called Moma. Her name was Anna Jackson, a light skinned woman who read a lot, had five children, but didn't seem to have a lot of patience with children. She delivered most of the babies in Ashdown in her day, worked with two white doctors, carried a doctor's bag, and was very busy with her work. She was often paid with a cow or pig and consequently had a good number of animals.

My mother's parents, Lonnie and Carrie Hawkins, were better known as Tunk and Jank, respectively. Even their kids called them these names. They were the proud parents of seventeen children. My mother was the third oldest child. She was and is called Hunene by her siblings, pronounced: Hun...neen with the emphasis on the last syllable. Another nickname situation.

At the age of thirteen months, my mother walked into a fire her grandfather had started, and her dress caught fire. She received severe burns to her lower abdomen. The local doctor said there was nothing he could do and that my mother would die. Her grandmother and mother had a different prognosis and worked on the burn daily. They nursed my mother back to health. Her mother slept with my mother on her chest. In retrospect, my mother knew God was looking out for her and had a plan for her life.

For her elementary years, she attended the Little River County Training School, a black (or colored) school. She worked in the cotton fields with her father and siblings from ages fourteen to seventeen. She said they took three watermelons to the fields with them: two to eat and one to wash their hands with, a sticky outcome.

She graduated from high school in 1952 as valedictorian of her class. She gave a speech, which she wrote with her father's help. She attended A&M in Pine Bluff, TX, with a major in secretarial science. After one year, she moved to Los Angeles to live with her father's sister, Aunt Cat.

She took a train to Los Angeles, which surely provided ample anxiety to her parents since she traveled alone at eighteen, and Jim Crow was alive and strong.

During that time, her train had a Pullman sleeper car. These cars were attended by the famed Pullman porters, who early on were recently freed slaves. In later years, blacks continued in this work. They were known for their strict attention to detail. At one time the Pullman Company was the largest employer of blacks in the U.S. These men wore their uniforms proudly.

About the train ride, my mother recalled only that she had to change trains in El Paso. In 1953, she rode in the colored car with few-to-no amenities. In El Paso, she drank from the "colored" water fountain and used the "colored" bathroom.

She married my father in 1954 and had two children in the next three years. She took classes at Los Angeles City

College and then worked at Mattel Toy Company for a few years.

The company was started in 1945 by Ruth and Elliott Handler and Harold "Matt" Matson. Initially they made picture frames, and after making dollhouses from leftover wood scraps, they decided to make toys. Although the parent company remains in El Segundo, CA, 80 % of the toys are made in foreign countries such as Thailand, Mexico, Indonesia, and China.

My sister and I liked that my mother worked for the toy company. Many of the toys made by Mattel were shown on TV. Barbie dolls and Hot Wheels were items of interest for children of those days.

After becoming a Seventh-day Adventist in 1965, my mother applied to licensed vocational nurse (LVN) school at the White Memorial Hospital in East Los Angeles in response to a flyer passed to her. This was a Seventh-day Adventist hospital that trained many nurses and physicians. It was a wonderful multiracial class of seven students; three Hispanic, two Caucasian, one Filipino, and my mother. She graduated from the program in 1966 as valedictorian.

She worked at the White Memorial Hospital a few years and then entered the registered nurse (RN) program

86

at Compton College and graduated in the top five in 1973. She then worked for years at the Martin Luther King Hospital in the Wilmington–Watts area of Los Angeles.

That hospital was built after the Watts riots in response to the '65 McCone Report, which outlined several health and other disparity issues within the black community in Watts. The most serious impediment to healthcare access was that the nearest hospital was ten miles from the Watts and South Central LA communities. The ground breaking ceremony was held in 1968, and the hospital opened in 1972. The hospital has been closed since 2005 due to a series of medical misadventures.

Because my mother was hospitable and a good conversationalist, we had frequent visitors to our Compton home. Several of her brothers stayed for months and years while they saved to buy their own homes, find a better-paying job, or got married. It was akin to having big brothers from my perspective.

Most worked for a meat-packing company, which meant that our house smelled like a barn after they returned home. I was not inspired to do this type of work. Only one of my mother's nine brothers works for a packing house now; however, he is a truck mechanic and no longer works with the animals.

My mother learned to sew and made clothes for herself and my sister. There was always a closet of fabric of many lengths and colors. After time, this closet spilt into other closets; the supply had exceeded the demand. The Singer sewing machine was heard often, including the early mornings and late nights. The sound was distinctive.

Martin Messier thinks so. He created the Sewing Machine Orchestra, using eight 1940s Singer sewing machines. The performance is mechanical and lacking in melody, yet interesting.

While my mother's machine never reached the big stage, it received plenty of use and after wearing out was replaced with a new and improved Singer model. The baton was passed on to my sister, and then two queens of the cloth resided in our family.

My mother is a great cook. She believes in eating healthy. When fast food became a substitute for home-cooked meals, my mother cooked for us. Most dinners included one or more vegetables. We ate Kentucky Fried Chicken, Jack-in-the-Box, and McDonald's, though not frequently. We never complained about it. We had heard stories of a dead mouse being found in a KFC box so there was great trepidation in going down this nutritional route.

My father drove us to Ashdown in the 60s to see my maternal grandparents. They lived in a house in a big field. Uncle Willie shot squirrels, and I watched him skin the critters. Amazing how easily the coats came off. After someone seasoned and cooked the squirrel meat, I had my first taste of squirrel. It tasted like chicken, but more salty. I haven't had squirrel meat since then, and no meat in the last twenty-two years.

One blogger had this to say about squirrel meat: "Squirrels from areas where corn and grain are their main food supply taste differently from the ones that eat mesquite nuts and desert blossoms. The best squirrels are those that eat mainly pecans and acorns; wow, what a flavor. "

On the other hand, a squirrel is a member of the rodent family. Although its primary diet consists of nuts and seeds, it may include other rodents, lizards, and insects. In Leviticus 11 God defined what was allowed (clean) and what was not allowed (unclean) for His people to eat.

My mother's family has remained closely knit and her parents lived to their late 70s and 80s. Consequently, I had the great opportunity to hear stories about the ancestors and to see how previous generations lived and functioned in society. My maternal grandfather gave me

89

papers showing his family tree that went back to the African man and woman, who were our first Hawkins ancestors in the U.S. This exciting discovery created a huge sense of personal value and a positive view of my family and its origins.

One summer while visiting my grandparents in Texarkana, TX, I interviewed them on video. Now I had a permanent recording of my grandparents' voices and appearance and how they expressed themselves. Sadly, someone stole my video camera with that cassette inside. I wish they would have left the film.

Alex Haley had done interviews to gather the information about his family tree to write the award winning book *Roots.*

Someone in the Hawkins family, in the distant past, had the foresight to gather this information and to pass it down several generations. While such history is frequently passed down by word of mouth, it was written in the Hawkins family. The knowledge of one's origins creates a sense of belonging and a responsibility to maintain family traditions, as well as, the integrity of the family.

My great-grandmother lived in Ashdown. I remember going to see her several times as a child. Her house was on a large plot of land, more than several acres. She had a few cows and other animals. I remember visiting her home at night and how dark it was inside. My great-grandfather was a very dark man. With the room dark, he was difficult to see. I remember the delicious sweet potato pie we sampled.

My mother grew up on a farm, as my father did, but their family stories were quite different. My mother was the one who hugged my sister and me and told us she loved us, two things my father didn't. He loved us; that was clear as time when on. He showed his love through action, not words, while my mother did both. She liked us to have dinner as a family, to attend church together, and to take vacations. An established family was important to her.

Our household had the typical rules, such as bed time, daily/weekly chores, and good home-cooked meals almost every day. It's amazing the disciplinary effect has on one: make your bed, wash the dishes, clean the bathroom, put out the trash, cut the grass, feed the dog, etc. Thanks, Mom!

My mother had no problem finding tasks for us around the house. With all that, we had enough play time to play. She was the major disciplinarian and the primary

91

administrator of spankings or simply *whuppin yo* butt. Belts and switches were the instruments of her choice. For those that might not know a switch is a long, thin tree branch with sufficient buds and twigs to leave whelps on the skin to remind a child to never even consider doing whatever he did to get the spanking in the first place.

Bibliography

1. http://answers.yahoo.com/question/index?qid=200904030 94222AA6XIeO

2. http://portable.tv/art/post/sewing-machine-orchestra/

Chapter 6 Fading Presence

Challenges encountered in peer relationships have been the area of public interest lately.

I experienced almost daily fights with a neighbor boy. I usually lost. It's remarkable that children fight one day and go out and play the next. He was bigger and stronger than me, and I was afraid of him. That didn't keep me from playing with him.

I got into a fight with him one time and saw my father cross the street to intervene. He didn't say anything, and his countenance showed no emotion. When I saw my father coming, I turned and gave the kid my best punch upside his head. I was amazed because he didn't move; he didn't wince or say one word. It was as though I hadn't

93

hit him. However, my hand let me know I had hit something hard.

I have reflected on what it meant to see my father coming to help me. The empowerment was massive and transforming. In my mind, I was suddenly taller, stronger, and fearless. What if my father had not come across the street? What if no one had come across the street? The fact that my father did made the result of the fight insignificant. This is empowerment that lives beyond the moment.

As usual, no discussion went on between my father and me following the fight. Today we emphasize talking and the importance of communicating better. We advocate better listening skills and, to a lesser degree, reading body language. These are important, but without a person being present, bodily or figuratively, these skills have no transformative power. Presence, attentiveness, involvement: these are the keys. My father's silent approach to this situation spoke loud and long. He was coming to help me. I did not immediately understand the full impact of his presence for some time.

Looking back, I've understood the 23rd Psalm better where it says, "I will fear no evil for thou art with me; thy rod and thy staff they comfort me." God's presence in our
94

lives should be powerful and empowering. And it can be! I was fortunate, unlike many youths today who have to face life's challenges alone. Thank God, the kids had not started carrying guns in the neighborhood then. Drive by shootings had not become an issue.

The last time I saw my childhood playmate was eight years ago. As I drove from my mother's house, I stopped at his house to say hello. I extended what I thought was a warm and enthusiastic, "What's up?" He stared at me and said nothing. He did not smile, wave, or tilt his head. He was motionless as he looked me in the eye. After moments of silence, I slowly drove off, thinking the incident was strange and wondered after all our time together as kids that our relationship had ended up like this.

Maybe no change had come in the relationship. He might have been dealing with something big enough to keep him from interacting effectively with the outside world. For unknown reasons to me, this was not the time for him to reminisce or share pleasantries. I had to remind myself that sometimes a change in behavior, opinion, lifestyle, status, or health may dictate that a relationship be put on hold and maybe only temporarily. A relationship change usually comes awkwardly, often without warning, sometimes with a verbal lashing, and sometimes without an explanation.

I have not seen or heard from him. I pray he is okay. Hopefully one day we can sit down to talk, have a few laughs, and express our gratitude to God for his deliverance from trials and other issues of this life.

My father talked about Charlie Parker, Earl Garner, Dizzy Gillespie, Duke Ellington, and other jazz greats. He had heard Charlie Parker play. He mentioned Charlie Parker patted his foot while he played. Now, YouTube can give us what we need to evaluate how and what Mr. Parker played. I listened to some of his jazz albums and wondered what on earth the musicians were playing. Their blazing flurry of notes made no sense to me. While I didn't know the technical terminology to describe the songs it was clear that there was a distinct difference in not having the hard beat, the thumping bass line, and the rich vocals of the popular R&B songs that I had been listening to.

While my father was aware of the Temptations, Four Tops, Supremes, Miracles, and other groups idolized in our community, he didn't buy their records or gravitate toward them or express disdain toward them.

He had albums by Charlie Parker and Lester Young, both saxophonists. These songs were on 72 rpm records. If you are of my vintage—old as dirt—then you remember those licorice-colored, scratchy-sounding, wobbly-turning, flat discs. You had to be careful when you put the needle onto the record and not scratch the record. And then pop! Crack! Hiss! Right? A few years later, I heard this sound used by rappers on their songs. How ingenious! An example of one man's garbage being another man's treasure?

A collection of these records would take up a large amount of space. Amazingly, today we store thousands of songs on IPods and the like.

Because of my father's influence, I started playing the saxophone in the fifth grade. In the ninth grade, I heard Hubert Laws flute version of "Amazing Grace" and Herbie Mann improvise on the flute. I wanted to play the flute.

While my father never gave verbal approval or encouragement to my hearing impaired saxophone practicing, he sat and listened. Again he was present. Silent but speaking loudly.

Each Sunday morning, I played softball with the church team. One Sunday my father watched the youngsters play the men of the church, and he ended up playing. He had decided to play, no doubt, from the persistent urging from the church men. He rarely watched the games, so to me, this was a treat.

We were playing at Gonzales Park in Compton. I played right field. I loved to run so the outfield suited me. I would have preferred left field any day. Michael Pennington usually played left field, and Major White, Jr. played center.

Seeing my father play any type of sport was a first for me. To see him with a glove on in right field seemed odd. When he came to the plate, he stood in the left-handers batting box. He was right-handed, so this was strange. My father's stance was like Pete Rose's, bent at the waist, but he was in no way a Pete Rose. He hit the first pitch deep into right field. The ball flew all the way to the fence, but I caught it. I thought he was lucky, and I was, too.

His next time at bat, he hit the ball again deep into right field. However, the ball didn't fall toward me. It continued over the fence for a homerun. I felt proud and excited. Although our team lost, seeing him hit the homerun was better than a win.

When my father drove us home, we were both silent. He never said one word about his homerun or me catching

98

From Karnack to Compton:

his fly ball. He said nothing about not playing since he was a kid, or what went through his mind when he came to the plate, or how the bat felt in his hands. He never even let on what he felt through his facial expressions.

I felt good because he was present, and we had represented the McCowan's well that day. He think he was as happy and proud as I was. It was a confirmation my father had athletic talents, a trait I was interested in. We'd had a father-son experience with a ball, a bat, and gloves.

In extolling the game, Walt Whitman, an American poet, said, "I see great things in baseball. It's our game— the American game. It will take our people out of doors, fill them with oxygen, and give them a larger physical stoicism. Tend to relieve us from being a nervous, dyspeptic set. Repair those losses, and be a blessing to us."

That Sunday, baseball provided a tremendous blessing to us.

My father never played baseball again with the church men. That was both interesting and sad to me. If I had hit a homerun, it would be hard to wait a week to play.

My father spent most weekday evenings sitting at the kitchen table with several books opened. He studied

99

electronics or math. He sometimes drew schematics (his words) of electrical circuits. He had several pencils, a slide rule, and a pad of graphic paper filled with numbers, symbols, lines, and unknowns to everyone else in the house. We had to stay out of the kitchen and not disturb him.

When I ran into difficulty with my homework, I hated to ask him for help, but he never complained. He stopped and patiently helped find ways to explain a simple concept to me. When I got the courage, I asked him to draw me an airplane.

His studying continued a few years and later transitioned from the scientific and technical to health-related topics. He read a magazine called *Prevention*. At the time, he talked about vitamins and cooked vegetarian dishes, things unheard of in our house, such as peanut loaf. We were initially leery of them. Why would anyone think of putting peanuts in a loaf? If one did, he should call it something else. But, it was very tasty and healthy.

My father smoked Tiparillo cigars. Yes, why would anyone interested in prevention and vegetarian cooking be a smoker? Well, for one it was more acceptable to smoke back then. And nicotine is powerful! The famous advertisement line for these slim "unisex" cigars with a white tip was "Should a gentleman offer a Tiparillo to a lady?" A popular, 1960s, TV commercial showed a woman at a party walking around with a box of smokes, calling out, "Cigars—cigarettes—Tiparillos." In the past I thought my father looked cool smoking cigars. No wonder.

Remember the Marlboro Man? If you do, you're old as dirt. The Marlboro Man rode that horse and looked fit, calm, and together. That was one of the most successful ads of all time.

The best known Marlboro Man was Darrell Winfield. He played the part over twenty years. At least four of these actors died of lung cancer. [1] Some said two of their horses died from second-hand smoke. Animal rights activists could weigh in on that one.

My father smoked on the front porch because my asthmatic chest grew tight from the smoke. No one in the house favored his habit or smelling the smoke. He said he could stop whenever he wanted to. He quit from time-to-time, but Mr. Nicotine intended to stay.

Nicotine is one of the hardest addictions to quit. None of the stop-smoking aids, such as nicotine gum, nasal spray, lozenges, and skin patches or medications such as bupropion hydrochloride (Zyban, Wellbutrin) and

101

varenicline tartrate (Chantix), were available when my father smoked. Nicotine patches were first available by prescription in 1992.

Back then, the primary driver in kicking the habit was a person's will. This remains true today for the will trumps any combination of stop-smoking aids.

I participated in Five-Day Stop Smoking programs, in which graphic pictures of diseased, black, scarred, and cancer-laden lungs were displayed along with people with missing mandibles or large, cancerous, mouth lesions. Fear of such personal calamities can be a strong motivator.

Loss is a greater motivator than gain is, according to the theory of loss aversion. And the use of prevention in kicking the habit often yields to the more powerful nicotine fit. Success in getting this monkey off the back is best sought by deciding to stop, setting a date, and doing it. Getting rid of caffeinated drinks, increasing water, fruit, and vegetable consumption, and asking for divine help should be included.

My father and I visited his oldest brother, Uncle Spend. He lived in a small house with his wife, Susie, in South Central Los Angeles. We saw him infrequently and primarily when I was quite young. The occasions were interesting and entertaining. Uncle Spend laughed heartily while telling stories. I didn't understand the humor, but this bigger version of my father was entertaining and it was good to see him have a good time.

After a few visits, I recognized some stories. My father sat quietly and respectfully, listening during the visit. He never talked about Uncle Spend. Their being only ten years apart I'm sure there were some stories of their youth they shared.

The last time my father and I visited Uncle Spend, he seemed different. He appeared taller, perhaps six feet - three. Of course, he wasn't. I had been used to seeing him sitting the other times. He had a good-sized Afro, and he didn't laugh as much. Where was the old Uncle Spend?

Aunt Susie let us in while Uncle Spend fixed food in the kitchen. He said nothing, just kept cooking. After awhile, he brought his food into the living room where we were and sat and started eating. Soon he spoke quietly with my father. I enjoyed hearing his rich, deep voice. He seemed pensive. He talked to my father for an eternity before he acknowledged my presence by turning slowly and asked how I was. He didn't say much else to me, but I was happy to see him. When my father and I were leaving, Uncle Spend stood on the front porch, saying,

"Y'all don't stay away so long." That was nice to hear. We needed to visit more often. However, we never returned. He passed away in 1987 at age 66. I wished that I hadn't been so quiet during those visits. I should have verbalized my curiosity about Uncle Spend and found out more about him.

My father worked for Space Technology Laboratories (STL), a company located on a hundred acres in Redondo Beach, CA, started by Simon Ramo and Dean Wooldridge. These two gentlemen had worked for Howard Hughes, but left in 1953 to form their own company. Ramo advised the architect to "lay out the buildings to offer every engineer a window with views of gardens and sculptures so they could 'think up big things.'" [2]

He also said, "I wanted it like a campus because that's where all the best minds were."

STL was responsible for developing ICB missiles under President Eisenhower, the Pioneer I satellite, and more than 195 spacecrafts. The company later became known as Thompson, Ramo, and Wooldridge (TRW). My father worked at TRW for seven years and then for a company called Teledyne in Los Angeles.

Kenny Knight and I (probably 12) went with my father to his job at TRW one night. I had never seen where my father worked. We played with the oscilloscopes and other electronic equipment in a very large room. There were all sorts of strange gadgets and machines in this room which looked like the robot repair shop from a Star Wars scene. Kenny was able to get the oscilloscopes make all kinds of noises.

Kenny was good at tinkering and fixing things. He owned an old Ford Falcon with a V8 engine with headers on it. Once in a while, he removed the mufflers and revved up the engine. He was "waking up the dead," as he called it. The sound was fairly powerful and impressive.

After leaving Teledyne, my father worked at Port Heuneme on missile guidance systems at the naval station, sometimes referred to as NAS Point Mugu. He drove fifty-six miles daily to Thousand Oaks and then caught a plane for a short ride to Port Hueneme. This daily trek didn't last long. My father told my mother that on all these jobs, he was the only African American. He had to deal with lack of promotions, isolation, and other forms of institutionalized racism. He returned home angry some days. At the time, my sister and I didn't know this because my parents didn't discuss it with us. Then in the

1960s, he wasn't the only one feeling the post-Jim-Crow inequality.

My father wrote my eighth grade graduation speech. His efforts yielded three pages on which that he never made a comment or recommendations on delivery to the audience. The latter was my mother's job. Every time she saw me in the house, she stopped me and made me say the speech. I was just reciting words. I'm not sure I really understood their in-depth meaning. Here is an excerpt from his work:

"To our principal, Mr. Nelson, our eighth-grade teacher, Mrs. Pritchett, our distinguished guests, parents, and friends. The eighth grade class wishes to thank each of you for your dedication and sacrifices in making it possible for us to attend a Christian school.

The 1969 graduating class had chosen its motto: "Victory through Christ." We chose this motto because we felt the words were appropriate for the time in which we lived.

Today abomination is all around us. We see it in starvation, violence, war, the misuse of drugs, and other selfish, sinful acts. In our country where we produce enough food to feed adequately every citizen, we find starving people. What is the reason for this apparent contradiction? It means the food supply is controlled by a handful of evil men. A shining star lies in the darkness: Christ, and through him, we shall be victorious.

Violence is abundant. In many homes, violence is portrayed on television. Newspapers are emblazoned with headlines of violence. The perpetrators of violence respect no man or God.

Recently, a church was destroyed by an arsonist in the city of Hawthorne. Another attempt was made to burn a church in Gardena. The life of the Rev. Dr. Marin Luther King, Jr. was taken by violence. Another minister was shot recently while he tried to protect a fellow man from harm. At times and in places, it is unsafe to walk alone because of violent robberies and molestation.

Though violence is rampant and out of control, we can overcome it and be victorious through Christ.

Starvation and violence are real and are in the forefront of many lives, but cannot overshadow war with its ravages and destruction. Wars have been fought, some of catastrophic proportion. Nations have developed weapons to rain down destruction and complete annihilation of other nations by war. Some nations desire to annihilate another nation. Each was to be the end of all wars. We shall be victorious over these impious nations through Christ."

My father's message is still relevant. I don't recall him writing anything else. I think he enjoyed this because he spent several days putting it together. It was his involvement in his kid's education. He never complained about "having" to do it. From my perspective, he took up the mantle and ran with it. That was his way.

I remember toward the latter part of his life telling him that I appreciated all he had done for me.

He responded, "I did what I was supposed to do." No fanfare, no preceding long sigh, no nodding of the head, or locking of the eyes, no statement about the challenges he faced. Just a simple one liner. All of his hard work and self-sacrificing summed up in eight words.

I was out of sync with this brief response. I kept silent, thinking he would say more. But nothing. I felt awkward. Maybe I was too soft by saying that. Maybe I picked the wrong time. When it became clear he would say nothing else, I was satisfied I had expressed my appreciation, though aware the expression in no way matched the sacrifice.

Saturday morning cartoons were a special treat. I rose early, filled a bowl with Kellogg's corn flakes, and parked myself on the floor in front of our fifteen-inch, black-and-white TV for hours. The corn flakes made the day, and everybody in the neighborhood ate them. Just flakes, a little sugar, and whole milk.

Today there are many cereal and milk choices. So fast-forwarding, you can have rice milk, almond milk, and soy milk for less fat and cholesterol and better health.

None of those were available in my youth. For the last ten years, I have used only vanilla-flavored, soy milk on cereal. Yuck! Actually it's pretty good. The corn flakes can be replaced with a variety of a nut, raisin, date, and brown sugar-laced concoctions that take twice as long to chew and digest. This stuff provides a serious workout for one's temporomandibular joint.

Saturday cartoons ended when my mother, my sister, and I became Seventh-day Adventists. Man, I missed my Saturday cartoons.

Although he never became a SDA, my father defended the biblical Sabbath against a Jehovah's Witness person at our front door. I stood behind my father as he talked to the visitor. When the discussion ended, my father closed the door and turned, surprised to see me on his heels. He immediately informed me that I was not to tell anyone of his discussion concerning the biblical Sabbath. At the time, I found the discussion and his desire for secrecy intriguing. He believed, but for whatever reason, he couldn't commit to keeping the Sabbath. Unfortunately, I obeyed and didn't bring it up again.

The biblical support of the seventh-day Sabbath is sound. Many are the non-biblical excuses for why it is no longer necessary to worship on God's-appointed, holy, blessed, and sanctified day. Some people call it a Jewish day, though the Sabbath existed before there was a Jew. Other people say the Sabbath was nailed to the Christ's cross when only the ordinances (not the Ten Commandments) were nailed to it, and that despite Christ's example, it doesn't matter on what day you worship. Revelation 22:14 says you must keep the commandments to enter heaven. Some have said the Ten Commandments were not referred to here and that only two commandments—loving God and loving your neighbor—were being highlighted. In Romans 13:8, 9, Paul tells us these two commandments are a summarization of the Ten Commandments, from which, Jesus said, nothing would be deleted until earth and heaven were no more. Certainly we will all choose our roads in this life and thereafter, but should we do so based on hearsay, tradition, and a mortal's philosophy?

110

My father quit working in electronics around 1972 and opened a liquor store in South Central LA at 49th and San Pedro. My mother pleaded with my father not to go into that business. She thought it was too dangerous. If he didn't get killed, he might become an alcoholic, she thought. No one in our immediate family was thrilled with his idea. We were used to seeing my father leave for work in a suit and tie, carrying a brief case, and sitting at the kitchen table working math problems. Becoming a liquor store owner seemed contradictory and unexplainable at the time. He had preached education and then was casting it aside for an occupation we thought he would never espouse.

Since I didn't communicate well verbally, I wrote him a letter, stating my opinion about his decision. He gave no response. Maybe my letter wasn't clear. Or maybe it was too difficult for him to respond. I never revisited the subject.

My father knew he needed change in his work environment. Enough said! How many seek a job change? Many! How many actually make a change? Far less. From his viewpoint, the door had opened, and he walked through it.

On Sundays, I visited his store on my way home from school. It always proved to be an interesting visit. One day I saw a man, named John, cussing out a telephone pole. He might have been on drugs or psychotic. He eventually hit the pole and had to have his arm put in a cast. I can tell you that the pole won that round but of the other subsequent times I haven't heard.

Another guy wore a couple coats, a couple shirts, and several pair of socks. He always jumped into the store. He never walked in like the other customers. Maybe he didn't like to hear the bell sound that occurred when someone entered the store or maybe it was his way of a grand entrance.

Other colorful individuals with stories of equal flair entered the store. My father told me he had to smack a guy multiple times with a two-by-four because he had stepped behind the counter and started a brawl. He mentioned he had to fire his pistol to discourage a threatening customer. All in a day's work? He became comfortable with these scenarios and laughed about them.

This side of my father didn't seem appropriate for him. I didn't know how to bring up the subject or where to go with the discussion. He seemed distant, in a faraway land that made him happy. He seemed less concerned about his family. What drew him to this situation laced with tension, chaos, and potentially dangerous and deadly liaisons?

My father stood behind the cash register with a big cigar in his mouth and an in-charge look on his face. I began to understand why he had left electronics engineering. He was the boss. The store was his; the products were his, as well as any decision regarding the store. He no longer had to deal with institutionalized racism. He did not have to wonder why he didn't get a promotion. The politics of the work place wasn't a source of anxiety. He had longed for an escape from the lonely microcosm of being one of few in the field of space technology in a post-Jim-Crowe era.

The benefit of the gamble of a career change seemed worth the risk. Once he had opened his store, he had finally arrived: a promotion to being the boss and not answering to anyone. What a relief! Similar to when you get your first car, it's usually used and may have a few dings, but it's yours, and you can drive where and when you want. Freedom! This was his Sojourner Truth, his underground railroad to the north, and he wasn't missing this train.

My mother's pleas fell on deaf ears. A man's long-desired freedom was her overpowering and stubborn opponent. Freedom was the opium because my father didn't seek a new car, clothes, or even vacations. He sought only to work at his store, a place he loved, but didn't love him, for it took his health, money, and life.

One morning my cousin, Donald, called to say my father had not come to work. Since he wasn't at home, I drove around town, looking for him. Only by grace, we found his truck in the middle of a side street, deep in South Central L.A. We found my father at a local jail. He said he had fallen asleep at the wheel. I think he had had too much to drink.

He stayed in the liquor store business about twelve years, working seven days a week. Over time, the day-to-day expenses and taxes exceeded the store's income. In 1988, he closed the store. A bitter pill. As captain, he had dutifully stayed on the ship until it sank. That which he had built with his time and countless hours of work, his hideaway, his source of income, his home away from home, and that which defined who he was, was now gone.

Then started a time of second guessing, bitterness, guilt, and blaming, followed by a redefining of himself
114

and a search for an alternate source of income. Thoughts of relinquishing control to an employer and conforming to the status quo were not what he cherished.

John Kennedy said, "Conformity is the jailer of freedom and the enemy of growth."

What would he do with no apparent employment options? My father was generally an optimist as he believed he could fix things himself and that life would get better. People say timing is everything; that goes for good and for bad, and for my father, this was definitely bad. His next phase of life proved to be more difficult than anticipated.

In the year my father closed his store, George H.W. Bush became President of the U. S., Nelson Mandela was still in prison, Atari became a Fortune 500 company with 493 million dollars of sales in 1987, and NBA stars, Kevin Durant and Derrick Rose, were born. Ironically the record of the year for 1988 was "Don't Worry; Be Happy" by Bobby McFerrin. The lyrics say, "In every life we have some trouble; when you worry, you make it double. Don't worry; be happy. Don't worry; be happy now." Even if these words became my dad's mantra, the song came and went and could encourage the listener only so much.

My father tried to study his way back into electronics, but much had changed. His area of expertise had surpassed his knowledge. He studied his old electronics books and worked equations like in the past. This went on for several months.

He realized he had changed, too. He was older, not as healthy, and not as motivated. He couldn't find his way back to electronics. The old adage "if you move, you lose" could have never been more true.

Many calculations he had done using a slide rule or an earlier calculator were now done by computers and in a much shorter time. He was no competition for the youngsters in his former field.

Someone once said, "It is better to be a young June-bug than an old bird of paradise." While he wasn't old, he was significantly older, a change that came too quickly.

Friends offered him odd jobs, one as a security guard. He didn't take the job. He had always had a well-paid job in electronics and was doing relatively well in the liquor store business until economics turned the tide against him. He had not planned for this situation.

The gray hairs and bifocal glasses came with regrets, anger, and depression. Alcohol soothed the pain temporarily, but thank God, he became hopeful and

116

relinquished this deadly foe. In his late-50s and on unfamiliar ground, he felt a sense of powerlessness and disenfranchisement that was of a great magnitude.

My mother recognized his depression, but he did not follow her recommendations to seek help or counseling. This was an expected response, considering his distrust of the "system," which was not unfounded with such travesties as the Tuskegee Experiment, a forty-year study in which 399 poor, rural, black men were denied available treatment for syphilis while told they were treated for "bad blood."

Harriet Washington has outlined other lesser-known offences in her 2007 book. *Medical Apartheid: The Dark History of Medical Experimentation on Black Americans from Colonial Times to the Present.*

My father's opinion of the healthcare system was also influenced by a botched appendectomy, which left him with an ugly, jagged scar. Furthermore, his view was that he wasn't crazy and didn't need counseling or a psychiatrist. He had fixed things all his life, so he would fix this.

My father developed prostate cancer in his late-50s. Prostate cancer represents one of the many health disparities facing the black community. The rate of

117

prostate cancer in black males is 226 cases per 100,000 males versus 145 cases in white males per 100,000 males. Black men are less likely to undergo screening for the disease. When the disease is discovered, it is often in an advanced stage, a more aggressive form, and more difficult to treat. The death rate is, therefore, higher in black men.

My father showed no emotions about the prospect of having his life cut short. Of course, the anxiety and the uncertainty about his survival and resiliency were present, whether they were voiced with anyone or not. There were no discussions of these concerns with his family. I think he believed he would conquer it as he had done with other problems in his life.

He decided on radiation therapy instead of surgery. Nerve-sparing, radical prostatectomy arrived in the early 1980s, but my father didn't want to take that route. He survived the cancer, but the radiation took its toll and added to the downward spiral of his life. While the radiation-emitting particles that pass through the body disable and minimize cancerous cell growth, they damage normal tissue as well causing some degree of impairment of normal bodily functions.

Not long after his cancer diagnosis, he began to read the Bible, signaling a realization that his new foe was too big for him to challenge alone.

Several years after he died, my wife was reading a Bible in our home and asked if I had underlined in Proverbs or if my father had. When I looked, I realized my father had done the underlining. I had seen this blue, ball-point pen underlining many times in the past. He had started in Proverbs and gone to the sixteenth chapter. It's interesting the things people consider important enough to underline in a book.

No other areas were underlined in his Bible. Perhaps this was as far as he got. He said he was reading the Bible. The way he said it suggested he believed he was onto something new with an anticipated reward. Later he said that it didn't work. I didn't ask what he meant by "work" and what he looked for when reading the Bible. I've been told the Bible has great literature. If that's all you're looking for, you will find it. However if you're looking for Christ—the way, the truth, and the life—you will find Him there, too. Unfortunately, I couldn't help my father with that perspective because at the time it wasn't "working" for me either.

In 1986, my father became a grandfather. We brought Brittany to see her grandparents when she was about 7 months old. After we visited awhile, my father drove off with Brittany without telling anyone or asking if he could take her. The problem could have been solved with a cell phone call, but this was before such technology.

He had taken her to see Aunt Bernice, his sister, about six miles away. Karlene was livid with my father. He didn't say a word, realizing he had used poor judgment. He was a proud grandpa who forgot to tell the mother or father he was taking his first grandchild for a ride.

In 1987, Karlene and I moved to Cleveland. It was bitter-sweet moving from our little, comfortable, 1100 sq ft home in our friendly neighborhood in Alhambra, CA. We didn't look forward to cold, snow-laden winters, but the opportunity for advancement had presented itself. Karlene's brother, Paul, and my father helped us with the driving. Brittany was eight months.

I rented a big truck that we packed with our belongings, hitched my 1982 Chevy S10 truck to the back, and headed out. Paul, Karlene, and Brittany rode in our car while my father and I rode in the rental truck. We used walkie-talkies to communicate along the drive. These brick-sized, consumer-grade devices were plagued with static and poor signals. The clarity of modern day cell phones is appalling in comparison to the walkie-talkies we had. A further challenge came with a screaming eight-month-old that was easier to hear than the one using the walkie-talkie. Being in that car seat for that distance was a challenge for this squirming baby. Using the available technology, we attempted to communicate bathroom, food, and sleep needs.

The four-day drive was not a pleasant trip with my father. He and I had a couple of disagreements interspersed with a generalized cold, silent atmosphere. I can't say exactly what was wrong. We were not melding, and neither tried to make the situation better. In retrospect this was very sad since the geographic distance between us would be great for an extended time.

Why is it that the rules and advice for handling relationships are often cast aside in families? In these times, intelligence and reason seem to be absent in those whom one would expect it.

Unfortunately, subjectivity and emotions ruled; nothing changed. I thanked him for helping us arrive in Cleveland and put him on a plane the day after we had arrived.

Today I would rewrite the script. Although the encounter was not enjoyable, he was present. If I needed him to return, he wouldn't refuse, nor would he complain. Having that type of security is big. It is a gift that should be appreciated, recognized, and not abused.

The last time I saw my father healthy was around 1991 when he and my mother visited us in Charleston, WV. We had wobbly kitchen chairs that he repaired without prompting. He drove to Lowe's and bought the necessary screws and repaired the chairs. Again, he said nothing from the beginning to the end of this self-appointed chore. And he didn't mention to anyone to see and compliment his work. This was his style of being there.

Over the following years, my father became progressively weaker and walked with a stooped posture. His physician treated him for Parkinson's disease, although that diagnosis was questioned. The weakness progressed to the point where he was unable to walk.

He was subsequently diagnosed with Shy-Drager's Disease, which is now called Multiple System Atrophy. This is a rare, multi-system failure disease of unknown cause. It affects men more than women. It can be confused with Parkinson's disease because the person develops problems with balance, bladder control, and erratic drops in blood pressure, which may cause the person to lose consciousness. These problems are due to degeneration of nerve cells in the brain and spinal cord. Respiratory failure, difficulty controlling emotions, trouble swallowing, and difficulty speaking may be seen in the final disease stages. Most patients die seven-to-ten years after developing symptoms.

This unfavorable prognosis was not initially believed by us, his family, because the neurologists waffled on a diagnosis. Nevertheless, progression of my father's symptoms confirmed the diagnosis. This was both alarming and depressing. He accepted his illness without major complaints.

He had two respiratory arrests at home, from which my mother resuscitated him. This had to be very frightening and stressful on my mother. Had she not been present, my father would not have survived these episodes. This highlights the importance of family members or someone working close to individuals at high risk for a cardiac or respiratory arrest to be proficient in cardiopulmonary resuscitation (CPR).

His last arrest was in October of 1994. He was taken to the Martin Luther King, Jr. Hospital in LA and placed on a ventilator.

I made the long trip from Charleston to LA. When I saw him, he was alert and responsive, lying in the ICU with a breathing tube. Not only was the breathing tube uncomfortable but humiliating for him. He had to ask himself, *how did I end up in this mess and how do I get out of it? And when will they remove this stupid tube so I can go home?* From his perspective, people were taking way tool long to address these issues he could not verbalize.

While daddy's immediate family comprised two nurses and a physician, the support team was not useful, and objective clinical acumen in this increasingly serious situation was lacking. Our youthful and strong father, husband, and provider was in trouble. His situation appeared like someone in the middle of the ocean on a raft with no oars to get to land.

I knew he was in trouble and that I might not see him alive again. With difficulty, I told him I loved him. He nodded.

I had never heard him tell me those words. Through a review of my childhood, his actions had said *I love you* time and time again.

I remember building the courage and forming the words with my mouth. I was relieved after saying it. Since

124

he couldn't verbally respond because of the throat tube, the nod had to be sufficient. That was the last time I saw him alive.

Mr. and Mrs. James Perry visited my father once a week to talk about Jesus and the Bible. This was loving missionary work, and I'm grateful. The last time they saw him, they said he cried, and they believed he had given his heart to God.

He could not respond verbally because of the respirator. I think he probably realized that he wasn't going to get better. The frustration of not being able to walk, feed himself, or turn himself in the bed must have been overwhelming.

The following day, April 11, 1995, he died suddenly at 63. He passed away with one child in Florida, the other in West Virginia, and his spouse on her way to see him, a scenario needing to be rewritten.

Such dying events should take place at home with loved ones paving the way, saying good-bye and whatever else needs to be said. The small consolation was the termination of his great suffering. Nevertheless, our loss was great and greatly felt. My mother's heart was broken with grief while the same force sent my sister and me into a bewildering semi-silence.

You never truly appreciate others' pain in the death of a loved one until you feel it yourself. For some, that road remains close by. However, some never leave it and remain crippled and bitter and unable to resume life as it was. Consequently, many fear death not for themselves, but for those left behind. The gift in this context is being able to prepare those left behind.

The typical Elizabeth Kubler-Ross stages of coping with death and dying (namely denial, anger, bargaining, depression, and acceptance) were out of order in my experience. There was no denial that he was going to die. Strangely, the anger wasn't there. It was overshadowed by confusion about how we, as a family, got into this situation. Had my father been exposed to a noxious chemical or an excessive dose of radiation in his travels within the space technology industry? Had he drank too much while in the liquor store? God only knows.

I had been bargaining with God on his recovery a long time, and the outcome made me feel like a failure. My prayers for my father's recovery had not been answered the way I wanted them. Perhaps I (we) had not prayed and fasted enough, or I was not living a good enough life for God to hear our prayers.

It was over, but my father's life was unfinished. He had dreams of accomplishing more. He still wanted to learn, and he wanted to be well. I felt sad because he had been an overcomer. Yet he was overcome. There was injustice to the situation. He had been cheated.

In his prime, he always worked to make the house look nicer, or to improve his health, or to learn a new subject. He believed that he could accomplish whatever he set his mind to accomplish. Just like the cigarettes he had smoked. He said he could quit whenever he wanted. He quit for periods, but he resumed the habit. But he finally quit for good, making good on his claim. In this life he was at the mercy of unconquerable foe, one rare and the other way too common, the Shy-Drager Syndrome and death.

Before his funeral, I found relatives taking his blue '67 Camaro. I had a hard time with that because it represented our time together. The Camaro was his favorite car. I had helped him rebuild the engine and fix other things on the car. I had driven the car to high school for a couple of years and had formed an attachment to it. This was the end of an era. I understood that things must change, but why so rapidly?

My mother asked me to say a few words at his funeral. I had not considered how difficult that task would be. I felt it a great honor to speak on my father's behalf for I could not recall his receiving any honors or recognition for his accomplishments. I had never publicly given him his due credit while he was alive. Sure, I had bragged on him as a kid and thanked him for making me do my homework and sending me to college, but I had never helped to let the light shine on him.

I was also terrified I would not complete this task because of grief. I put something together. I broke down and cried when I tried to present it to my mother. As I listened to what I said, my personal loss became overwhelming. My father wasn't coming home on earth again. I wouldn't hear his voice anymore. I wouldn't see him again for the rest of my life. These were all new experiences that I yearned to reverse. I had finally experienced one of life's daily occurrences and was grateful to have escaped until now. I had joined the ranks of the millions.

Sometime after the funeral, going through old boxes at my mother's house, I came across old, computer, floppy disks my father had used. My mother told me to look at them in case my father had left a message for us or had

128

recorded words to fill the gaps of communication in our home life. Nothing was present. This communication issue was interesting.

Sometimes we assume somebody is not communicating if he doesn't answer us in the methods we choose for them. It's surprising how much is "said" in the absence of words. Hand gestures, facial expressions, silence, whistling, singing, body postures, and grunts speak volumes when applied with the right timing and if the one "spoken" to can interpret it.

The huge communication gap between us got better over the years. As I've discovered, this was not unusual for fathers and sons in the time I grew up.

Although he never uttered the words, it wasn't an issue because I felt his caring and concern. He was the one who was most adamant about my sister and me practicing the piano daily and getting good grades. When we were sick, he got up at night to give us medicine. He read us stories each night when we were young. That's not to say that my mother was not committed to the same goals. These were roles my father took.

A poignant paradox has been the Grand Canyon-sized gulf between what religionists have taught and what their main textbook, the Bible, teaches about death. The

129

newspapers' obituaries drive home the current beliefs of the deceased being immediately raptured to heaven, a concept refuted in the good book. Those attending funerals often say, "Absent from the body, present with the Lord" in support of the immediate "home-going."

However, 2 Corinthians 5:8, says, *"We are confident, I say, and willing rather to be absent from the body, and to be present with the Lord."* Paul is saying he'd rather not have to die, but to be translated to be with the Lord. He is not addressing the state of the dead.

In Job 14:10-14, the writer asks the question, *"...man giveth up the ghost, and where is he?"* Then proceeds to answer it in verse 12 by saying, *"So man lieth down, and riseth not till the heavens be no more..."*

When Lazarus died, Jesus and Martha had this exchange noted in John 11:23, 24, *"Jesus saith unto her, thy brother shall rise again. Martha saith unto him, 'I know that he shall rise again in the resurrection at the last day.'"*

In 1 Corinthians 15:51-54, it's made clear that immortality begins at Jesus' second coming.

Ecclesiastes 9:5-6 says *the dead know nothing*, and verse 10 says they do nothing.

Peter said in Acts 2:29 that *"...David...is both dead and buried,"* and in verse 34, *"For David is not ascended into the heavens."*

In John 14:3, Jesus said, *"And if I go and prepare a place for you, I will come again, and receive you unto myself; that where I am, there ye may be also."* And when he returns, it is to retrieve His dead and living followers, according to 1 Thessalonians 4:16, 17. The Bible is consistent on this issue.

So when ones dies, the heart stops beating, blood quits flowing to the brain and other organs, followed by a cessation in bodily functions. People take their last breath, and as per Ecclesiastes 12:7, that *breath or spirit returns to God, who gave it.* If you are one who is familiar with and embrace the biblical narrative, you can appreciate the importance of accepting the teachings as they are given.

In 1 Timothy 4:1, we are told that *...in the latter times some shall depart from the faith, giving heed to seducing spirits, and doctrines of devils.* We can expect that these seducing spirits will take human form, according to 2 Corinthians 11:14, 15. If one firmly believes the deceased goes directly to heaven, then it is easier to believe that the deceased can be active in the affairs of this world and can communicate with us. These beliefs are contrary to biblical doctrines and greatly increase one's susceptibility to other false beliefs.

From Karnack to Compton:

Chapter 7: The Seed of Legacy

In closing the story about Jack McCowan it is notable
through large monetary gifts, the donation of property and
items of significant value, the erection and naming of
buildings and streets, the delivery of powerful and
compelling speeches, and other means, we remember and
honor the worthy folk who walked amongst us, paved the
way for us, and saw us take our first steps. Legacy is part
and parcel of all whether we're destined to be known by a
handful or the world at large. Though we can paint a
lovely picture of how we want to be remembered,
onlookers may embellish it or see only the cracks,
blemishes, and the stray colors that no mere mortal can

erase. Some make profound efforts to create a lasting and often fantasized legacy of themselves. But the tried-and-true pattern includes extreme self-sacrifice, humility, and overcoming great odds.

It is both interesting and amusing that those seeking public office appear blind to their own litany of deeds that reveal character failure. Corruption seeks power as does power corrupt. While honor is too often post humus, the fruits of one's legacy are usually more readily seen.

The seed of legacy is a full set of chromosomes bearing generations of personalities, character tendencies, a physique, intellectual prowess, and health predilections. These may plague or positively reward us and may be the foundation of fame and fortune for the excess of us who seek it. Closed-door socioeconomics may nullify the seed of legacy and serve as a great source of negative behavior and minimized goals. When the door of socioeconomic opportunity opens wide, a greater probability is that the seed of legacy will grow and blossom and with less frustration, intrusions, road blocks, and derailment.

Conversely, this seed of legacy and any accompanying negative socioeconomics may have an inescapable downward pull although those with means may be blindly convinced that with a good work ethic alone, success is entirely achievable. When such is the case, what can possibly negate such powerful influences?

Consider this: *And God is able to make all grace abound toward you; that ye, always having all sufficiency in all things, may abound to every good work: (As it is written, He hath dispersed abroad; he hath given to the poor: his righteousness remaineth forever. Now he that ministereth seed to the sower both minister bread for your food, and multiply your seed sown, and increase the fruits of your righteousness;) Being enriched in everything to all bountifulness, which causeth through us thanksgiving to God.* (2 Corinthians 9:8-11)

A bare-bones summary of these words: God is able to help us abundantly in every good work. We do our part, and He will do His.

Jack McCowan was all about letting seeds grow and did his best to cultivate them, water them, and eliminate the weeds.

Let us all let the seeds grow.

Bibliography

1http://www.thedailybeast.com/newsweek/2008/05/10/o-father-where-art-thou.print.html

http://www.tshaonline.org/handbook/online/articles/sim02

2. http://www.bookrags.com/history/popculture/alka-seltzer-bbbb-02/

3. http://toys.about.com/od/a/fpclassictoys.htm

4. African: the encyclopedia of the African and African American experience.

Kwame Appiah and Henry Louis gates, Jr, 1999, Basic Civitas Books, 10 East 53rd Street, New York, NY 10022-5299.

5. Theophillus, http://www.helium.com/items/279078-why-major-league-baseball-should-bring- back-the-negro-league, April 16, 2007.

6. http://www.cdc.gov/nchs/fastats/lifexpec.htm

7. http://health.drgily.com/american-longevity-adventist.php

8. http://vip.hyperusa.com/~davislt/Church%20Attendance%20-Life%20Expectancy.htm

9. "Religion and Health Study Progress." *Adventist Health Studies Report 2008* **V**: 5. 2008

10. Gary E Fraser, American Journal of Clinical Nutrition, Vol. 70, No. 3, 532S-538S, September 1999.

11. Joan Sabaté American Journal of Clinical Nutrition, Vol. 70, No. 3, 500S-503S, September 1999.

12. Tara Parker-Pope, New York Times, Health, Sunday, January 29, 2012.

13. Andrew J. McDermott, Mark B. Stephens, Fam Med 2010;42(4):280-4.)

14. Remember When 1931, Seek Publishing.

15. http://www.ergopage.com/wpa_murals.html

16. http://www.ralphmag.org/AN/wall-to-wall.html

17. http://www.whitehouse.gov/history/presidents/hh31.html

18. Kosar, Kevin R. (2005). "Disaster Response and the Appointment of a Recovery Czar: The Executive Branch's Response to the Flood of 1927" U.S. Library of Congress, Congressional Research Service, pp 9–10. Washington D.C.

19. http://www.bls.gov/news.release/empsit.nr0.htm

20.   http://www.eeoc.gov/eeoc/newsroom/release/8-11-05.cfm Tyson foods

21. 12. Register, Charlene Film History: An International Journal, Volume 17, Number 2005, pp. 113-124 (Article), Published by Indiana University Press.

http://muse.jhu.edu/journals/fih/summary/v017/17.1regester.html

19358856R00080

Made in the USA
Lexington, KY
15 December 2012